Driving
While
Black

Driving While Black

HIGHWAYS, SHOPPING MALLS,

TAXICABS, SIDEWALKS:

HOW TO FIGHT BACK

IF YOU ARE A VICTIM OF

RACIAL PROFILING

Kenneth Meeks

Broadway Books

New York

BROADWAY

Broadway Books titles may be purchased for business or promotional
use or for special sales. For information, please write to:
Special Markets Department, Random House, Inc., 1540 Broadway,
New York, NY 10036.

BROADWAY BOOKS and its logo, a letter B bisected on the diagonal, are
trademarks of Broadway Books, a division of Random House, Inc.

Visit our website at www.broadwaybooks.com

The author wishes to thank The National Association for the
Advancement of Colored People for authorizing the use of the sample
letter that appears on pages 73–74.

Library of Congress Cataloging-in-Publication Data
Meeks, Kenneth, 1963–
Driving while black : highways, shopping malls, taxicabs, sidewalks :
how to fight back if you are a victim of racial profiling /
by Kenneth Meeks.— 1st ed.
p.   cm.
Includes bibliographical references.
1. Discrimination in law enforcement—United States.
2. Discrimination in law enforcement—United States—Prevention.
3. Searches and seizures—United States.   4. Traffic violations—United
States.   5. Minorities—Civil rights—United States.   I. Title.
HV8141 .M39 2000
363.2'32—dc21   00-028932

FIRST EDITION

Designed by Chris Welch

ISBN 0-7679-0549-0

04   10   9   8   7   6   5

I dedicate this book to Glenna, my wife and *consigliere*.

Contents

Contents   ix

Introduction

I n 1942, over 120,000 Americans were stripped of their businesses and their homes and incarcerated for the duration of World War II. They had committed no offense. They were convicted of no crime. They were suspected, subjected to curfews, arrested, had their property confiscated, and finally imprisoned because of the color of their skin and their national origin or the national origin of their parents.

The internment of Japanese Americans in 1942 was an egregious example of what can happen when skin color and national origin are substituted for evidence and become, by themselves, a basis for suspicion and punishment. But it was not the only egregious example.

During the time of the internment, Jim Crow laws and

formal racial segregation existed in the American South and was so reified that virtually no one could imagine it ending. A nation that had long ago learned to tolerate and accept Jim Crow laws that victimized African Americans was well prepared to accept internment that victimized Japanese Americans.

Today, the internment of American citizens of Japanese descent is nearly universally recognized as something shameful, an act of war hysteria and racism. Similarly, few today are prepared to defend the formality of Jim Crow laws.

But on our highways, on our streets, in our airports, and at our customs checkpoints, skin color, irrespective of economic class, is once again being used by law enforcement officials as a cause for suspicion and a sufficient reason to violate people's rights.

This book documents the extent of racial profiling. The statistics speak for themselves, eloquently. But this book is not a sermon; it does not preach. What it does—very effectively—is to put information into the hands of those whose rights are violated, and provide them with the means to resist, to fight back, to protect themselves. It is a handbook more than a call to arms, a manual of instructions and self-help more than a political tract.

This is important, because the defense of individual rights always begins with intelligent, strategic resistance by those whose rights are violated. The history of individual freedom in America, and how it developed, begins with the Bill of Rights, with the establishment of an independent court system to enforce it, and with the availability of lawyers to bring crucial cases to court, often without charge. But, above all, the history of individual rights in America is a history of individuals who fought back, who invoked the principles of freedom and who by their struggles established principles of freedom.

The Fourth Amendment, which limits the authority of the police to search citizens, was itself a product of such a struggle. During the late eighteenth century, American colonists were infuriated by the widespread practice of British customs inspectors entering their homes at will, even if they had no evidence of a violation, and ransacking their belongings looking for contraband. These searches were deeply resented, and resulted in a growing demand that no search should be permitted unless the government could show specific reasons—*evidence*—for suspecting a particular individual.

That demand was rejected by the colonial courts and by British governors. But the resentment grew and, some say, was a leading cause of the anger that led to the American Revolution and, ultimately, to independence.

The Bill of Rights, including the Fourth Amendment, was an early result of independence. And the Fourth Amendment, requiring search warrants based on specific evidence, was a direct outgrowth of the resentment against general searches. Today, that resentment is echoed by the victims of racial profiling.

But resentment is only the beginning of change. What is needed is a method for converting resentment to an effective strategy of resistance. This book provides to people who want to stand up for themselves and defend their rights the means to do so. Resistance, of course, does not automatically guarantee a remedy. But accepting the violation of rights is the surest way of guaranteeing that the violations will continue. Hence, the importance of this book.

If those early Americans who resisted the warrantless

searches of their homes by British soldiers could have seen this book, they would have recognized the problem and applauded the advice. *Driving While Black* should be on everyone's bookshelf, and perhaps in everyone's glove compartment as well.

—IRA GLASSER
Executive Director, ACLU
February 9, 2000

Driving

While

Black

Part
One

CHAPTER 1

Understanding Racial Profiling

n 1959, a ten-year-old boy named Sam was riding his new bicycle through the racially mixed town of Hempstead, Long Island. It was a beautiful spring day for the little boy, who had waited since his January birthday to ride his birthday present from his mother. It was the hottest bike out on the market at the time—a Lemon Peeler.

Sam was down the street from his home when suddenly a police car pulled up beside him.

"Where did you get that bike?" one of the policemen asked as he rolled down his window.

"My parents gave it to me for my birthday," the little boy answered.

"You're lying," the policeman snapped. "This bike is too expensive for you to have."

"Get off the bike," commanded the other officer. They got out of the car and surrounded the little boy. "We got a report that this is a stolen bike."

"Not this bike," Sam responded. "My mother bought me this bike."

"You stole that bike."

"No I didn't."

"You live around here?"

"Are your parents home? We're going to take you home and ask your folks."

The two white officers placed the bicycle in the trunk of the police car, put Sam in the backseat and drove him home. It was a scary ride for the boy. He had never been treated like a criminal before.

Sam's mother answered when the police officers knocked on the door.

"Did you buy your son this bike?" one of the officers demanded.

"Yes, and what did my son do?" she asked.

"We got a report that the bike was stolen."

"I bought him this bike. Why are you harassing my son?"

Instead of getting into an argument, the officers took his mother's word and walked away without an apology to Sam or his mother. Sam hadn't done anything illegal, and there was no reason for the police to stop him. So what had happened?

THE DEFINITION

This is a classic example of racial profiling, the tactic of stopping someone only because of the color of his or her skin and a fleeting suspicion that the person is engaging in criminal behavior. It's generally targeted more toward young black American men and women than any other racial group, although Asians, Hispanics, and even young whites with long hair and a hip-hop flair about them get profiled more every day. It doesn't matter if there is "probable cause" or not in many instances. A police officer or a security guard or anyone in a role of authority can detain and question people, and some believe that racial profiling is a justified form of law enforcement and detective work, while others vehemently disagree. Whether or not you believe that racial profiling actually exists, the practice has been proven over and over again. The attorney general's office of New Jersey, the state whose practices sparked national attention on the subject, acknowledged that racial profiling did exist among its highway state troopers. And the latest edition of Webster's New Collegiate Dictionary includes an entry for the term. It defines racial profiling as "the mass police policy of stopping and searching vehicles driven by people of particular races."

Racial profiling may be a relatively new term, but it's definitely an old concept. Tracey Maclin, a professor at Boston University School of Law, says that the problem of "driving while black" can trace its historical roots to a time in early American society when court officials in cities like Philadelphia permitted constables and ordinary citizens the right to "take up" all black persons seen "gadding abroad" without their master's permission. This means it transcends law enforcement and includes everyone—people like store clerks, bank tellers, security guards, and even taxi drivers.

We must ask ourselves: Is racial profiling a subtle form of legal prejudice? Or is it a legitimate way to stop crime before it takes place? And what are the consequences of racial profiling for African Americans—or Asians, or Middle Eastern Muslims, or even Hispanic and Latinos—as a matter of local, state, or federal government practice? In 1976, the U.S. Supreme Court supported the actions of the U.S. Border Patrol agents who selected cars for inspection in Southern California partly on the basis that drivers were of Mexican descent. The Supreme Court maintained that since the intrusions by the U.S. agents on selected drivers were "quite limited" and only involved "a brief detention of travelers during which all that is required . . . is a response to a brief question or two and possibly the production of a document," the practice was upheld. And recently in upstate New York, the U.S. Court of Appeals for the Second Circuit ruled that police officers did not violate the Constitution when they stopped every black man in Oneonta on September 4, 1992, after a seventy-seven-year-old white woman said she had been attacked in her home by a young black man. The woman said the burglar had cut himself on the hand, and the three-judge panel ruled that the police sweep of blacks was constitutionally permissible and not racially discriminatory because the police were acting on a description that included more than just the color of the alleged assailant—that is, the cut on the hand.

The controversy surrounding racial profiling is intense. In the national spotlight are two New Jersey state troopers, John Hogan and James Kenna, both of whom were indicted on September 7, 1999, on attempted-murder and assault charges resulting from a shooting during a routine traffic stop on the New Jersey Turnpike in 1998 that left three of the four unarmed young black and Hispanic men involved seriously wounded. The troopers were also indicted earlier that year on nineteen misdemeanor charges of falsifying their activity logs to conceal the disproportionate number of minority drivers they were accused of stopping on the highway.

From a legal point of view racial profiling is tricky because it can be difficult to prove. Seldom do investigators recover a smoking gun with fingerprints on it. This is why a national movement has been launched by politicians of color and civil-rights leaders to mandate that law-enforcement agencies keep statistics of whom they are stopping, questioning, detaining, and searching. Black leaders say it's the only way to be sure that people of color are not being stopped because of their skin. Robert Wilkins, a Washington, D.C., public defender, said he had discovered in his lawsuit with the American Civil Liberties Union (ACLU) against the Maryland State Police that on Interstate 95 in Maryland, 70 to 75 percent of the people being pulled over and searched were African Americans, although they made up only 17 percent of the total drivers. Unfortunately, only recently have a handful of police agencies started to keep records of traffic stops according to race, gender, and age. Several attempts in Congress to make a federal law requiring law-enforcement agencies to keep such records on all traffic stops were defeated in the Senate. We'll talk more about that later.

Racial profiling is tricky in other areas, too. On one hand, the courts say that large groups of American citizens should not be regarded by law-enforcement officers as presumptive criminals based upon their race. On the other hand, the courts acknowledge that facts should not be ignored simply because they may be unpleasant. Randall Kennedy, a professor at Harvard Law School, explains that society can't pretend that blacks and whites commit crimes or are victims of crime in exact proportion to their respective percentages of the population. "Statistics abundantly confirm that African Americans—and particularly young black men—commit a dramatically disproportionate share of street crimes in the United States. This is a sociological fact, not a figment of the media's (or the police's) racist imagination." In recent years, for example, victims of violent crime report blacks as the perpetrators around 25 percent of the time, although blacks constitute only about 12 to 15 percent of the nation's population. This raises an interesting question that must be addressed, too. One answer is to say racial profiling is wrong when race is the only factor for stopping a person but not when race is taken into consideration alongside a host of other observed criminal behavior. Is the answer really that simple?

To some degree, we all participate in our own form of profiling, our own form of assuming that a person is a particular way only because of that person's appearance, race, or manner of dress. By no means are law-enforcement officers the only ones who profile. Security personnel in the local shopping mall are potential racial profilers. The salesclerk behind the counter in the local clothing store is a potential racial profiler. Taxi drivers engage in racial profiling every time they drive past a black person hailing a cab to pick up a white person down the street, and if you've talked to any young black New Yorker, you'll know that experience happens to someone, somewhere every night. Just ask actor Danny Glover, who in the fall of 1999 filed a formal complaint with New York City's Taxi and Limousine Commission because of one too many such experiences. When does this cross over into criminal behavior?

It doesn't matter if the year was 1808, 1909, 1959, 1970, or 1998, prejudices and stereotypes among the races will always exist. According to the Honorable Renee Cardwell-Hughes, of the Philadelphia Court of Common Pleas, the act of stopping minority motorists who drive luxury cars in the assumption that they are using the highways to smuggle drugs, or stopping an individual under the assumption that he is a criminal is a violation of the Fourth Amendment to the Constitution—"the right of the people to be secure in their persons, houses, papers and effects, against unreasonable searches and seizures, shall not be violated, and no Warrants shall issue, but upon probable cause, supported by Oath or Affirmation, and particularly describing the place to be searched and the persons or things to be seized." Judge Cardwell-Hughes strongly disagrees with the decisions handed down by the Supreme Court in several important cases involving racial profiling. She says that the Fourth Amendment's protection is shrinking. Law-enforcement officers use a profile known as CARD, an acronym for class, age, race, and dress. Any lower-class, young black person wearing baggy jeans, a T-shirt, and a backward-facing baseball cap can expect to be stopped by a police officer or followed around upon entering an upscale department store in an upscale neighborhood. Unfortunately, this describes a hundred thousand young people on any given day in any given city. And as more and more young white people adapt the dress and style of today's inner-city black kids, they, too, will become a small minority of white people who get racially profiled.

Stopping people of color along Interstate 95 in New Jersey on the suspicion that they are trafficking in illegal drugs has been going on for years. But New Jersey should not be singled out. We focus on New Jersey state troopers in this book because they have been notorious in the practice of racial profiling. By examining that state, we understand racial profiling as it exists in the rest of the country.

BIBLIOGRAPHY

- "The Fourth Amendment: Origins and Original Meaning," by William J. Cuddihy (1990), an unpublished dissertation, provided by Professor Tracey Maclin, Boston University School of Law.
- "Suspect Policy," by Randall Kennedy (September 13 & 20, 1999); *The New Republic* (p. 33).
- "2 New Jersey State Troopers Indicted in Turnpike Shooting," by Ronald Smothers (Wednesday, September 8, 1999); the *New York Times*.
- "Breathing While Black," by Bob Herbert (Thursday, November 4, 1999); the *New York Times* Op-Ed page.

CHAPTER 2

Driving While Black

THE NEW JERSEY TURNPIKE

amuel Elijah remembers June 1994 like a bad four-car collision. He was driving his white Mercedes on the New Jersey Turnpike just outside Trenton around eleven o'clock one night, heading home from a day's work of renovating a client's house in Willingboro. He was tired but very much alert. This had been his fifth or sixth time making the hour-and-a-half commute back to his Staten Island home. He was driving between fifty-eight and sixty miles per hour.

He had just driven beneath an underpass when he noticed a state trooper hiding on the other side of the viaduct. Reflexively he checked his speedometer again, and just as he had been several miles back, he was still driving fifty-eight miles per hour. He didn't think he had any reason to be worried. Yet it was only natural that he checked his rearview mirror for the police car, and that's when he saw it pull out. There were no flashing lights, so Sam wasn't concerned. He kept driving within the speed limit, looking back through the rearview mirror.

Sam, a dark-skinned black man, took in a deep breath of summer night air blowing through his open car window to remain calm. Once again he checked his rearview mirror. The police car continued to close in to within thirty feet. Sam made a mental note of how long the police officer followed him. Five minutes had passed, and the police car was still tailing him, driving so close that he could almost feel the officer's breath down his neck.

What's the story with this guy? Sam wondered. *Is he going to stop me or what?*

Sam continued driving steadily in the middle lane of I-95, and the police kept following him. Five minutes turned into ten, and for a split second he considered getting off at one of the exits. But since he was now driving exactly fifty-five miles per hour and breaking no law, why should he turn off?

After fifteen minutes of being followed at close range, Sam started to get annoyed. Finally he'd had enough. He pulled off into the emergency lane, and the squad car pulled up directly behind him. Sam got out and walked over to the police car. Inside was a lone white officer.

"Why are you following me?" Sam asked.

"Get back in your car," the police officer commanded over the cruiser's loudspeaker.

Without saying another word, Sam returned to his car. And that's when he noticed the lights of another police car. The second squad car pulled up in front of his Mercedes, penning in Sam's car. A third pulled up directly behind the first squad car. Blue flashing lights sliced through the night.

When the other officers had parked, the white police officer who had been following him finally got out and walked up to Sam's open window.

"What's all this about, officer?" Sam asked.

"Driver's license and registration," the officer demanded.

"What did I do?"

The police officer didn't answer. He only took Sam's documents back to the squad car, and while Sam waited, the three officers converged behind Sam's car, discussing something among themselves. When the first officer returned to the 1980 white Mercedes driven by the dark-skinned man, he shone his flashlight in Sam's face.

"Your eyes are red. Have you been drinking?" the officer questioned.

Sam didn't have a clue to what was going on.

"Did you have any drinks today?" he asked again.

"No," Sam answered. "I've been working all day. I'm tired."

"What kind of work do you do?"

"I do construction work."

The officer was apprehensive. "Your driver's license is from New York. What are you doing down here? Where are you coming from?"

"I'm coming from Willingboro," Sam answered. "I was going home until you guys came down on me. I don't understand, why are you stopping me anyway? I wasn't speeding."

"You look like you've been drinking. Step out of the car. I want you to take a sobriety test."

"A sobriety test?" By now Sam was pissed. He was a married family man with a three-year-old son and just wanted to get home. "I didn't drink anything. I've been working."

Nonetheless, the officer put him through the routine test. Sam felt humiliated having to walk a straight line and touch his nose with his eyes closed. Though the highway was virtually deserted that time of night, the few cars that passed stared at him as though he were a criminal. It was clear to Sam's sober mind that the officers were fishing for something incriminating. But they didn't have anything.

After a few more minutes of the officers talking among themselves, the lead officer returned to the white Mercedes and gave Sam back his license and registration.

"You can go," he said with a hint of disappointment in his voice.

In the matter of half an hour, Sam had been violated and abused, and he felt helpless. He was angry, and he had a right to be. Yet there was nothing he could do about it at the time but get back behind the wheel of his car and watch two of the three squad cars drive off. No amount of summer air could stop the rage that boiled in his veins from having been the victim of the New Jersey State Police's abuse of power.

When Sam finally collected his wits, he put his car into drive and slowly pulled back onto I-95. The same officer pulled out behind him, continuing to follow him for another five minutes or so before finally exiting the turnpike.

It would be another four years before Samuel Elijah learned that he was not the only black man driving a luxury car to be pulled over by the New Jersey State Police.

The *Village Voice* would publish in the summer of 1998 an article on claims that New Jersey troopers were routinely stopping black motorists, chronicling similar stories of abuse of power. Coincidence? Sam doesn't think so. And as comforting as it would be years later when the New Jersey Assembly held hearings on racial profiling, it was of little comfort on the night that Samuel Elijah was stopped on the side of the road on his way home from work.

WHAT SAM WOULD DO IF HE WERE STOPPED AGAIN

When Samuel got home that night, he told his wife, who was a criminal attorney, about the experience. They brainstormed on an idea that if he should be pulled over again, he would follow certain procedures. And though he was never stopped again, the idea that the couple came up with was a good one for anyone caught in a similar situation.

First, take note of the time of day. Is it morning? Afternoon? Evening? Late at night? Be sure to make a mental note of the exact time. Most cars are equipped with some kind of clock. Keep it set properly. Knowing the precise time that the police encounter begins might become important later.

Also, take note of your surroundings. Where were you stopped? Look for landmarks that will help you identify your location. If you're on a highway, note the mile marker or the exit number. Make a mental note of any advertising billboard that helps you pinpoint your location. If you're in the city, what street were you stopped on? What part of town? What is the racial makeup of the residents in the neighborhood? Familiarize yourself with what's going on around you. If at all possible, get the names and phone numbers of people walking around in the neighborhood or, better yet, the people who witnessed your police encounter. You might have to call them to testify for you should the encounter get out of hand.

Sam and his wife agreed that he should not have gotten out of the car. To a police officer, this connotes danger. When the police officer approaches your car, upon his request show him your driver's license, registration, and proof of insurance. Don't make any sudden movements, and if you have passengers in your car, tell them to remain still, quiet, and polite. Keep in mind that a police officer does not need a warrant to search your car, especially if the officer has "probable cause" like smelling alcohol on your breath or detecting evidence of drug use.

And if the officer demands that you get out of the car, you should take your keys and lock the car. That way, if you're asked to step away from the car, no police officer will have access to your car without your permission. If the police want to search the car but do not have probable cause, they would have to follow proper legal procedure and first obtain a search warrant.

Of course, if you volunteer to open your car, the police can search everything inside, including personal handbags. Recently the court upheld the practice that if a passenger has a closed, personal handbag that does not belong to the driver, that handbag can also be searched without the passenger's permission.

Now, if the police forcibly search your car, they have violated proper legal procedure. Without just cause, they don't have a right to search the vehicle, and your locking the car eliminates the possibility of something illegal being planted in the car to show "just cause."

If it is required that you sign the traffic ticket, do so, *even if you disagree with it.* You have the right to dispute this later in court. And once you have the ticket and the police officer releases you from custody, immediately write down everything that happened: what you were doing, how you were driving, where you were going, what time you were stopped, the officer's name; what he (or she) looked like, what was said to you, what questions you were asked, the officer's manner of addressing you, and whether he wanted to search your car. Remember everything you can, because within minutes of any type of experience we all start to forget the little details that make up the larger picture. In essence, document everything. It's probably a good practice to keep a small notepad and pen in your glove compartment specifically for police encounters.

The National Association for the Advancement of Colored People (NAACP) issued an action alert regarding the Traffic Stops Statistics Study Act—H.R. 1443 in the House and S. 821 in the Senate (or "Driving While Black" bill)—calling for people living within the minority community to contact elected representatives from both the House of Representatives and the Senate and demand that they support this legislation. The bill, introduced by Congressman John Conyers (D–MI), passed the House on March 24, 1998, but was defeated in the Senate prior to the 105th congressional session. In order to become a federal law, the bill had to pass the 106th Congress—including passing the House again, and the Senate—and be signed by the President of the United States. As of fall 1999, the Senate refused to pass legislation. President William Jefferson Clinton promised his support.

In fact, on June 9, 1999, President Clinton ordered a memorandum to the Secretary of the Treasury, the Attorney General, and the Secretary of the Interior to begin addressing the problem of racial profiling. He mandated that these federal agencies design and implement a system to collect data at all levels of law enforcement to define the scope of the problem and keep statistics on the race, ethnicity, and gender of those who are being stopped or searched (see the chapter entitled "National Acknowledgment"). The study keeps track of identifying characteristics of individual stops, including the race and ethnicity of the individual, as well as age, whether a search was conducted, and whether an arrest was made as a result of either the stop or the search. Limited studies indicate that 72 percent of all routine traffic stops occur with African American drivers, although blacks make up only about 12 to 15 percent of the driving population. (To date only three states—New Jersey, Connecticut, and North Carolina—have passed similar legislation. A California bill passed overwhelmingly in the state legislature on September 12, 1999, but was vetoed by the governor. Other states still pending include Illinois and Massachusetts.)

Leaders of color are asking Americans to show support for this bill by calling the House of Representatives in Washington, D.C., and asking to be transferred to your senator or congressperson's office. The Capitol switchboard's phone number is (202) 224-3121.

The NAACP also urges people of color to write to: The Honorable (name of senator); U.S. Senate, Washington, D.C. 20510; or to your representative: The Honorable (name of representative), U.S. House of Representatives, Washington, D.C. 20515. To send e-mail, visit www.senate.gov, or www.house.gov. And remember to contact both of your senators.

The nation's largest organization of police executives [the International Association of Chiefs of Police (IACP)] will oppose any federal effort to require officers to collect race-related data on people they stop for traffic violations.

> —"Police Chiefs Resist Race-Related Tallies,"
> by Kevin Johnson and Gary Fields,
> *USA Today* (April 8, 1999)

Did You Know?

- In the mid-1990s, a New Jersey Superior Court judge, the Honorable Robert E. Francis, found that racial profiling was legal.
- CARD is an acronym used to distinguish how people justify racial profiling. It stands for class, age, race, and dress. Anyone fitting a certain economic class, within a certain age group, born to a particular race, and wearing hip-hop (or street) gear will likely be profiled as a potential criminal.
- A professor at the University of Pennsylvania Law School and a civil-rights lawyer in Philadelphia found similar racial disparities in traffic stops along I-95 just south of Philadelphia. The professor won

a class-action lawsuit against Tinicum Township, where the stops were being conducted.

- The American Civil Liberties Union (ACLU), who together with the Maryland State Conference of the NAACP Branches, filed a class-action lawsuit against the Maryland State Police over race-based stops of black drivers on I-95, established a complaint form for victims of racial profiling. Their Web site is www.aclu.org/forms/trafficstops.html.
- The ACLU's California affiliate established a hotline for victims of racial profiling at (877) 392-7867.

CHAPTER 3

National Acknowledgment That Racial Profiling Exists

obert Wilkins, chief of the special litigation program inside the public defender's office in Washington, D.C., remembers the drive back from Chicago the weekend he attended his grandfather's funeral in May 1992. Wilkins and his wife had rented a car with his uncle and first cousin. They decided to drive all night Sunday to get back into Washington on Monday morning, so everyone could return to work. It was an emotional trip. While passing through western Maryland on Interstate 68, their rented car was stopped by a Maryland state trooper. Robert's cousin was driving.

Outside, it was drizzling. Inside the car, most of the

family slept. But when they were pulled over, instead of issuing his cousin an immediate ticket, the officer ordered the driver outside of the car. The white officer and Robert's cousin stood at the rear of the car for several minutes before Wilkins and his uncle got out to investigate. It turns out the state trooper was pressing Robert's cousin to sign a "consent to search" form.

Robert identified himself as an attorney and said that they knew what their rights were. He immediately told the officer that his family didn't want to be searched.

"You don't have to sign the form," Robert told his cousin.

"If you got nothing to hide, then what's your problem?" the trooper asked.

"I thought we have the right not to be searched and detained by the police, and we want to exercise that right like anybody else."

"Well, this is routine, and everybody consents."

"Well, that may be the case," Robert told the trooper. "I can't speak for what everybody else does, but we don't want to consent."

"If you don't want to sign this form, then you're going to have to wait here for the dogs to be brought."

Shock went through Robert as he wiped rain from his face. He informed the state trooper of a 1985 Supreme Court decision called *United States* v. *Shark* that said if an officer wants to detain a citizen, that officer has to have "reasonable articulate suspicion" that the citizen is involved in narcotics activity.

"I don't think you have any 'reasonable articulate suspicion,' because we haven't done anything wrong."

"We have a problem with rental cars and drugs on the highway," the trooper answered. "That's why this is being done."

Robert didn't understand. The Maryland state troopers couldn't possibly stop every rental car traveling down the highway. And since when did driving a rental car create reasonable suspicion?

"This is routine, and this is the way we do things."

Robert Wilkins, who had to be in court the next morning defending a case, now wanted only to be left alone and be on his way. It was going to be a long drive, and they were trying to beat Monday morning's rush-hour traffic to get home first before going on to work.

"Is there a way we can accommodate the trooper?" his uncle asked. "What is it you want to search?"

"I want to open your trunk, take your bags out, and go through your bags and everything else in your car."

Robert said that was out of the question. They were on the side of the road, in the middle of the night, and it was raining. If they emptied the car in order to accommodate the officer, all their luggage would get soaked.

"You better go get your dog, then," his uncle answered.

The dog eventually arrived with three accompanying police cars. Flashing lights pulsated through the misty night. Robert Wilkins and his family, en route from a family funeral, now had to endure a half-hour police search while the German shepherd went around the car, jumping on the hood, sniffing the windshield wipers, the headlights, the taillights, and the hubcaps. This wasn't just a walk-around-the-car-and-sniff procedure; the dog performed a thorough search. It even jumped up on the side of the car to sniff along the edges where the windows retract into the door and crawled under the car.

Meanwhile, the family stood in the rain as passing cars slowed down to stare, rubbernecking the scene, pointing at them as though they were criminal suspects caught in the act. It was a humiliating, degrading, dehumanizing experience.

The dog never barked. In the end, Robert's cousin was issued a $105 ticket, and the family was allowed to leave.

The following morning Robert immediately contacted the ACLU. They and a local law firm in Maryland agreed to represent Robert Wilkins and his family. Wilkins's case was a good one at the time because he was a Harvard Law School graduate who specifically cited to the Maryland state trooper the Supreme Court case that said the officer couldn't search the car. The troopers didn't find drugs, and Robert had documented everything—the names of the officers, the badge numbers, the license-plate numbers— writing down as much information as he could. In fact, the only thing he didn't get was the name of the dog.

Robert Wilkins's legal team believed that he had a strong civil-rights case, and he sued. During the discovery process, Wilkins and his lawyers learned that two weeks before Robert was stopped, the Maryland State Police had distributed a criminal-intelligence report to the barracks where the troopers were stationed. The report explained that blacks were bringing crack cocaine into the area, that they were driving rental cars—especially rental cars with Virginia registrations—and that they were driving early in the morning or late at night. But to show how contradictory it was, the same report said that most perpetrators were driving alone—or with a lot of people. Two weeks prior to the

Robert Wilkins incident, the Rodney King decision had been issued, and Los Angeles was rioting against police brutality. The nation as a whole was beginning to reexamine the police's relationship to the minority community.

Robert Wilkins's case was eventually settled in January 1995. The settlement not only provided a small amount for damages and attorney fees but it mandated that the Maryland State Police adopt a nondiscrimination policy and that they no longer use race as a reason for stopping people except when there was a particular description for a particular suspect. The Maryland State Police also agreed to discipline any officer who violates the nondiscrimination policy. But more important, they were required to keep records and statistics of who was being searched, either by consent or by the drug-sniffing dogs, according to the race of the individuals. They were required to keep such statistics for several years and give the data to Robert Wilkins's legal team and the federal judge presiding over the case. Robert's legal team also discovered that on I-95, between 70 and 75 percent of the people who were being searched were African Americans. This prompted the lawyers to conduct their own study of driving up and down I-95, keeping notes and focusing on demographics (a category not covered under the settlement). The study showed that 17 percent of the drivers were African Americans, yet they were 70 to 75 percent of the people who were being searched. So naturally the legal team expanded the scope of the study to determine who was violating traffic laws. They conducted a complicated study consisting of driving up and down I-68 and I-95 and counting who was speeding and who was violating traffic laws, and they found that 93 percent of all drivers on I-95 were violating some form of traffic laws. There was no difference between blacks or whites as to the percentage of who was breaking the traffic laws.

And how is this for another discovery?

Robert Wilkins's legal team found in its study that when the Maryland State Police actually found drugs, it was in the same percentages among whites and blacks. According to Robert, "When they searched a hundred blacks and a hundred whites, they found drugs exactly the same number of times, but they were searching seven hundred blacks for every one hundred whites, so the arrest statistics made it look like seventy percent of the people being arrested for drugs were African American, and then they use those statistics to justify focusing on the African Americans."

The "Criminal Intelligence Report"

This is the complete text of the "Criminal Intelligence Report" as distributed to the Maryland State Police Department. Wilkins's legal team discovered the existence of this report and provided a copy to people who attended the 1999 NAACP 15th Annual Lawyers CLE Seminar held in New York, July 9–11, 1999.

Criminal Intelligence Report
State of Maryland
Maryland State Police
Date: 04/27/92
Hour: 1700
Telephone: (301) 759-4660

Agency/Assignment: 18-D.E.D./ Allegany
County Narcotic Task Force:
- Current Investigation
- Highly Reliable
- Investigation
- Surveillance

Subject: Armed drug traffickers in Allegany
County, Maryland. Police Officer Safety

Details of Report: Confidential, Confidential,
Confidential

Allegany County is currently experiencing a
serious problem with the incoming flow of crack
cocaine. The majority of the crack cocaine is going
directly into Cumberland, and is beginning to sur-
face in the Frostburg and Westernport areas as well.
The dealers and couriers (traffickers) are predominantly black males and black females.

The drug traffickers are utilizing Interstate 68
and Route 51. Although some of the deliveries
of CDS are made during the daylight hours, the
majority of the drug shipments arrive in Allegany
County in the late evening and early morning
hours. Route 51 appears to be the more preferred
mode of travel. The traffickers will be coming from
east of Cumberland heading west into Allegany
County. If a trafficker is stopped traveling towards
Cumberland, they will have a quantity of crack
cocaine in their possession. If they are traveling
east, they will most likely have very little, if any,
drugs, but will be carrying large sums of money.

The drug traffickers will utilize a variety of
vehicles, usually standard size automobiles. Please

pay particular attention to rental vehicles and especially vehicles displaying Virginia registration. The traffickers will usually travel with two or more people in the car, however, several are known to travel alone.

The drug traffickers feel that police officers are much less apt to search females as thoroughly as males, therefore, be aware that any females found riding in the trafficker's vehicle are probably concealing the drugs on them, usually in their panties, bra, etc. Also, for the same reason, the females have been known to carry handguns for the traffickers.

Through intelligence sources, it is a known fact that some of the drug traffickers that are coming into Cumberland are wanted in various jurisdictions for a variety of criminal offenses. They will utilize various methods to provide false identification if stopped by the police. Also, many of the drug traffickers have extensive criminal records including homicide, armed robbery, along with various drug convictions and other criminal-related offenses.

CAUTION! Several of these people coming into Cumberland have been involved in shootings and several have commented that they will not hesitate to shoot a police officer if necessary. The weapons of choice are .380 and .45 automatic handguns.

If you conduct a motor vehicle stop and it appears that the occupants are potential drug traffickers, use extreme caution and wait for a backup unit before taking additional enforcement action. DO NOT let the occupants know that you have requested a K-9 drug dog, or drug task force inves-

tigator, or backup units. This might alarm them
and create a potential dangerous situation for you
while you are alone with them. Make it appear that
you are simply conducting a routine traffic stop.

If a vehicle stop is made that possibly relates to
the above information, please obtain identification
information from all occupants of the vehicle and
provide it to the Allegany County Narcotic Task
Force. If an arrest is made, please notify the task
force so that we may respond as part of an ongoing
investigation we are conducting.

Approved By: Section Commander

THE NEW JERSEY STATE ATTORNEY
GENERAL'S "INTERIM REPORT"

In 1999, in the wake of a national outcry by civil-rights
officials and leaders of color against the police practice of
racial profiling across the country, the New Jersey state
attorney general's office initiated an investigation into the
allegation that its state troopers engaged in the practice.
We follow New Jersey specifically because that state led
the nation in accusations of racial profiling and then
attempted to cover up the disproportionate number of
minority drivers who were being stopped by a method
known as "ghosting," in which license-plate numbers of
white drivers who were not stopped were being written
down on the police activity logs. People of color were not
the only victims of profiling; many white drivers who
weren't stopped might find it unsettling to know that their
license-plate numbers might be logged in official police

records without their ever knowing it. This is virtually no different from someone's using your Social Security number without your knowledge. It's a subtle form of the state's stealing your identity.

On April 23, 1998, Daniel Reyes, twenty-one, Leroy Jermaine Grant, twenty-four, and Rayshawn Brown, twenty-one, were shot eleven times while traveling in a van en route to a basketball tryout (the driver of the van, Keshon Lamonte Moore, twenty-two, was not shot). The van was stopped by troopers. During the stop, the gear slipped out of park and started moving. The troopers opened fire. The New Jersey state attorney general commenced an intensive investigation into the shooting, which eventually led to the indictment of two of the officers, John Hogan, twenty-nine, and James Kenna, twenty-eight, on falsifying official records and later on attempted murder charges. In a report entitled "Interim Report of the State Police Review Team Regarding Allegations of Racial Profiling," Attorney General Peter Verniero and First Assistant Attorney General Paul H. Zoubek scrutinized a situation the minority community had charged for decades—state troopers targeting minority motorists only because of their skin color. Verniero, who in 1998 became the state's supreme court justice, refuses to comment on issues of racial profiling.

The attorney general was unprecedentedly daring. Verniero wanted a comprehensive review of the state police on issues such as racial profiling and shooting protocols. His office investigated the issue for four months before he officially admitted that New Jersey state troopers were regularly engaging in racial profiling. The office also acknowledged that although the racial-profiling issue has gained state and national attention, the underlying conditions that foster disparate treatment of minorities have existed in New Jersey for decades. And although the attorney general's office expressed that a majority of state troopers were honest, dedicated individuals committed to enforcing the laws in a fair, professional, and impartial manner, there was clear evidence that minority motorists have been treated differently than non-minority motorists during the course of routine traffic stops on the turnpike. The report found that the problem of racial profiling was real, and not simply imagined.

Understand that the attorney general's office was operating under a slightly different definition of "racial profiling," broadly defining the term to encompass "any action taken by a state trooper during a traffic stop that is based upon racial or ethnic stereotypes and that has the effect of treating minority motorists differently than non-minority motorists." This definition included the action of a police officer who orders a driver or a passenger to step out, subjecting the person to questions that are not directly related to the specific vehicular violation for which officers stopped the car, summoning a drug-detection canine to the scene, or requesting permission to conduct a consent search of the vehicle and everything in it. According to the attorney general's office of New Jersey, data suggest that as of 1999 minority motorists were disproportionately subjected to car searches, a count that reaches nearly eight out of every ten consent searches conducted by troopers assigned by Morestown and Cranbury state police stations that involved minority motorists.

The attorney general and the governor of New Jersey have since condemned the practice of racial profiling by anyone. In May 1999, New Jersey prosecutors dropped drugs and weapons charges filed against twenty-one black or Hispanic motorists because John Hogan and James Kenna, the troopers who either stopped or arrested them, were later indicted on charges that they racially profiled black and Hispanic motorists and then tried to falsify records. Hogan and Kenna made these twenty-one arrests months before they fired on the four young black and Hispanic men in a van en route to the basketball tryouts. They were arraigned on charges that the troopers falsified official documents by reporting the black and Hispanic drivers they had stopped were white. Defense attorneys representing the twenty-one motorists publicly expressed that any conviction of the minority motorists who were arrested by Hogan and Kenna could be overturned. Because the two troopers were essential witnesses in each of the twenty-one cases, and because they were charged with lying on official documents, the officers lacked the credibility necessary for a successful prosecution. An attorney for two of the twenty-one defendants told the press he was denied access to evidence showing that the two officers engaged in profiling.

The New Jersey attorney general's office's handling of these twenty-one cases involving state troopers John Hogan and James Kenna was seen as the result of ongoing investigations into allegations that state troopers have regularly singled out black and Hispanic motorists for traffic stops and drug searches. Attorney General Peter Verniero publicly promised that any officer who violates the civil rights of (or racially profiles) minority motorists would be indicted and subject to the disciplinary procedure of criminal prosecution, taking full advantage of New Jersey's official misconduct laws. The attorney general proposes remedial legislation to provide prosecutors with additional statutory tools to deal with oppressive police misconduct as well.

In general, there are no clearly spelled-out, written standard-operating-procedures manuals or formal training curricula for a highway-patrol officer to refer to when electing to stop a vehicle. This gives officers an extraordinary amount of discretion. The state trusts that officers will exercise reasonable judgment in deciding whom and whom not to stop, particularly because in this vast "universe of vehicles," according to Robert Wilkins's study for his lawsuit against the Maryland state troopers, virtually every car operated on the highway violates some aspect of the law and is therefore subject to lawful detention. And this creates its own problem. Troopers who conduct themselves without accountability have the potential to continue any abusive behavior they've started. Therefore, it was made clear by the attorney general's office that as a matter of policy, race, ethnicity, and national origin should not be used at all by Jersey troopers in selecting vehicles to be stopped or in exercising discretion during the course of a stop (other than in determining whether a person matches the general description of one or more known suspects).

The American Civil Liberties Union

In 1993 the ACLU initiated a class-action lawsuit against the Maryland State Police (MSP) on behalf of Robert L. Wilkins. A court settlement in the lawsuit required that the MSP maintain computer records of all motorist traffic stops, searches, and arrests. In

November 1996 the ACLU in Maryland asked the court to hold MSP in contempt of court because it had violated the earlier court decree. The ACLU contended that the MSP continued a pattern of race discrimination in drug-interdiction activities carried out along the I-95 corridor. Invited to sift through the data, Temple University professor of psychology Dr. John Lamberth provided extensive expertise in statistics that helped the ACLU introduce its traffic-violation survey into court records.

The ACLU explained that 5,741 cars were observed in a "rolling survey" designed to identify the race of the motorists during the course of forty-two hours. The ACLU observers were able to identify the race of the motorists 96.8 percent of the time. They noted that 973, or 16.9 percent, of the cars had black drivers. Four thousand three hundred forty-one, or 75.6 percent, of the cars had white drivers. According to the civil-rights organization, over 93.3 percent of the motorists being surveyed were violating traffic laws and could easily have been stopped by state police officers.

Between January 1995 and September 1996, the MSP reported searching 823 motorists on I-95, north of Baltimore. Six hundred sixty-one, or 80.3 percent, were black, Hispanic, or some other racial minority. Six hundred, or 72.9 percent, were black. The ACLU argued that the growing problem with racial profiling has escalated during the early 1980s as a direct result of the "war on drugs" (see "When Profiling Works").

Amnesty International Investigates
the United States

While only a minority of the thousands of law-
enforcement officers in the United States engage in
deliberate and wanton brutality, Amnesty International discovered that too little was being done to
monitor or check officers who do persistently cross
the line and engage in police brutality or abuse. In
essence, the organization found evidence that racial
and ethnic minorities were disproportionately the victims of police misconduct, including false arrest and
harassment.

In 1992, the United States approved its participation to the following human-rights treaties that
contain standards and protections relevant to the treatment of individuals by law-enforcement officials. They
include:

• *The International Convenant on Civil and Political
  Rights.* This maintains that every human being has
  the right not to be arbitrarily deprived of life and
  the right to freedom from torture or ill treatment.
  Article 26 states that all persons are entitled without any discrimination to the equal protection of
  the law and that "the law shall . . . guarantee to
  all persons equal and effective protection against
  discrimination on any grounds such as race, color,
  sex, language, religion, political or other opinion,
  national or social origin, property, birth or other
  status.

- *The International Convention on the Elimination of All Forms of Racial Discrimination.* This maintains that states must eradicate racial discrimination, including in the judicial system, and guarantee "the right to security of person and protection by the state against violence or bodily harm, whether inflicted by government officials or by any individual group or institution."

Launched in October 1998 with a 150-page report entitled "Rights for All," a yearlong campaign waged by Amnesty International revealed a "persistent and widespread pattern of human rights violations" taking place within the borders of the United States. For more information, call the organization's toll-free number, (800)-AMNESTY. However, for a detailed report of the organization's campaign, visit the Web site www.rightsforall-usa.org, or visit Amnesty International's Web site, www.Amnesty-USA.org. You may also contact any of the following offices:

National Headquarters
Amnesty International USA
322 Eighth Avenue
New York, NY 10001
(212) 807-8400

United Nations Office
777 UN Plaza, 6th floor
New York, NY 10017
(212) 867-8878

Regional Offices
Northeast Regional Office
58 Day Street
Davis Square
Somerville, MA 02114
(617) 623-0202

Southern Regional Office
31 Ponce De Leon Avenue, NE, Suite #220
Atlanta, GA 30308
(404) 876-5661

Midwest Regional Office
53 W. Jackson, Suite #731
Chicago, IL 60604
(312) 427-2060

Mid-Atlantic Regional Office
600 Pennsylvania Avenue, SE, 5th floor
Washington, D.C. 20003
(202) 544-0200

Los Angeles Office
9000 W. Washington Boulevard, 2nd floor
Culver City, CA 90232
(310) 815-0450

Refugee Office
500 Sansome Street, Suite #615
San Francisco, CA 94111
(415) 291-9233

BIBLIOGRAPHY

- This chapter is based on the personal appearances of Robert Wilkins and Reginald Shuford, staff attorney for the ACLU, at the "1999 NAACP 15th Annual Lawyers CLE Seminar" held in New York, July 9–11, 1999, and follow-up interviews.
- "Interim Report of the State Police Review Team Regarding Allegations of Racial Profiling," by New Jersey Attorney General Peter Verniero (New Jersey Department of Law and Public Safety, April 20, 1999).
- "United States of America: Race, Rights and Police Brutality," published by Amnesty International (September 21, 1999).

CHAPTER 4

Your Legal Rights During a Traffic Stop

A cross the United States, highway-patrol officers are constantly making split-second decisions when determining whom to pull over for a traffic violation. When over 90 percent of all cars are violating some traffic law, the discretion an officer uses to stop someone is based on experience, training, the specific circumstances, and the risk. A "routine" traffic stop for speeding is handled differently than a traffic stop based on an initial suspicion that the motorist is driving under the influence of drugs or alcohol, and both of these traffic stops are handled much differently than a "high risk" traffic stop based on the suspicion that a driver, or a passenger, has committed a serious crime or a felony.

We all get pulled over for traffic violations. White people

get pulled over. Black people get pulled over. So do Asians, Latinos, young people, old people, new drivers, and experienced drivers. Those who've never been pulled over should consider themselves very fortunate. For this reason, anyone who owns a driver's license should be aware of his or her rights as a motorist. And for parents of teenage motorists who are into the hip-hop culture—traveling with a carload of buddies with long hair, baggy clothes, loud music, and a carefree attitude—we should all take a moment to review our rights before we let them get back behind the wheel. Just as people of color get pulled over for "driving while black or brown," so do white teenagers who travel either with black friends or with other white kids who associate themselves with black culture. And white kids who drive around town listening to loud rock or heavy-metal music are profiled, too.

We will examine specific points during the course of a routine traffic stop that state troopers must make, a decision that carries legal consequences for both the troopers and the motorist. It would be impossible for this book to represent a comprehensive description of the laws regarding arrest, search, and seizure. For that, we suggest you take a law class. But this chapter gives you a basic understanding of the legal standards and criteria with which state troopers must comply at various stages during traffic stops both within city limits and along interstate highways. Keep in mind that each state has its individual laws regarding the rights of motorists during a traffic stop, so it would be wise to familiarize yourself with your state's laws.

THE "TERRY" STOP

Under the terms of the Fourth Amendment, a police officer may not order a pedestrian or a motor vehicle to halt or
remain in a particular place unless the officer has reasonable, articulable suspicion that a criminal offense has been
or is being committed. Referred to in legal terms as the
"Terry" stop, or an "investigative detention" as established
by the case *Terry* v. *Illinois*, this type of stop has a limited
purpose: It is a brief, on-the-scene investigation that allows
an officer either to confirm or to dismiss any original suspicion of criminal activity that justified making the stop. If
this brief detention takes too long, the officer must escalate
the encounter into an "arrest," which requires him or her
to present facts or evidence constituting full "probable
cause" that a crime such as drunk driving has been or is in
the progress of being committed.

In legal terms, there is a distinct difference between the
"reasonable, articulable suspicion" standard that officers use
to justify an investigative detention (a "Terry" stop) and the
higher "probable cause" standard used to justify an arrest.
When a motorist is pulled over for a traffic stop, the police
officer immediately gives his "reasonable, articulable suspicion" of unlawful activity, such as telling the driver that he
or she was speeding, or was weaving through traffic, or
failed to stop at a stop sign. In cases of traffic stops, the officer relies on his senses, or his radar, or whatever relevant
information he has at his disposal. But not all state patrol
officers have radar in their car, so the law allows patrol officers to travel along with traffic at a rate of speed greater

than most traffic so that the trooper isn't limited to observing the same motorists for any extended period of time. Or the patrol officer can take up a stationary position and observe vehicles as they pass by. Or officers can follow behind or "pace" a vehicle to reliably ascertain the vehicle's speed or observe the driver's behavior, such as in Samuel Elijah's case.

THE "TAKEDOWN" LIGHTS

According to the New Jersey State Attorney General's office, speeding or weaving between lanes is the most common reason cited for stopping a vehicle. When an officer decides to make an official stop, he or she will activate the police vehicle's overhead "takedown" lights to attract the motorist's attention and order the car pulled over. It is customary for the officer to position the police vehicle directly behind the detained vehicle in a manner that will protect the detained vehicle from being struck by other traffic. (Although individual states operate within their own procedures for traffic stops, the customary practices described here for New Jersey are fairly standard among all fifty states.) When both cars are at a complete stop, standard operating procedure requires that before exiting the police vehicle, the officer must "call in" the stop. The officer provides the dispatcher at the police communications center with a description of the detained vehicle and its passengers and driver. When Samuel Elijah got out of his car to approach the police trooper behind him, he was ordered to return to his vehicle because at this initial stage of the police encounter the motorist is not allowed to exit his vehicle and approach the state trooper's car.

Only after the traffic stop has been called in will the trooper "cautiously" approach the detained vehicle. If the trooper is riding with a partner, one trooper will normally approach the driver's side (depending on traffic) while the other positions himself on the passenger side to monitor any activities taking place among the passengers. State troopers, as do most police officers, make it standard procedure to look into the car, to watch for suspicious movement, or to be alert as to whether the driver or any passenger demonstrates extreme, unusual nervousness. They're always watchful for weapons or any contraband out in "plain view" or for any attempt to mask the odor of illegal drug use.

The trooper has the right to ask a motorist to shut off the engine or to request that the driver and passengers keep their hands within view. At this point the officer will ask the driver to provide certain documents: a driver's license, vehicle registration, and—depending on what state the stop occurred in—proof that the vehicle is insured. When the driver has provided the documents, the trooper will return to his vehicle and radio the information to the dispatcher, who will initiate a motor-vehicle background check to determine whether the driver's license has been revoked or suspended, whether the vehicle is properly registered or reported stolen, or if the driver is wanted for any outstanding warrants.

The state trooper has the right to ask certain, limited questions specifically relating to the driver's itinerary, such as where the motorists are traveling from and where are they headed. These are considered routine questions in the course of a trooper's search for any discrepancies or anomalies suggesting that the drivers and the passengers are lying, which might in turn suggest criminal behavior. These series of polite questions are also intended to determine whether or not the driver is coherent, thereby indicating that the driver might be under the influence of alcohol or drugs. Again it should be noted that individual states have specific laws pertaining to when an officer can and cannot ask a driver and any passengers out of a car. For instance, in every state across the country state troopers can order a driver to step out of the vehicle if the trooper believes the driver to be intoxicated. A trooper can also request the driver out of the car in order to monitor the movements of the driver if the trooper feels that his own safety is at risk. New Jersey state troopers by law are not permitted to order passengers out of the car unless the officer is aware of "articulable facts warranting heightened caution." As a general rule, police officers during a routine traffic stop are not permitted to conduct a frisk or protective pat-down unless the officer has a reasonable, articulable suspicion that the person to be frisked is carrying a weapon. This must be more than a hunch, for the officer must be able in court to point out specific facts that led to the suspicion that a particular individual was carrying a concealed weapon.

JUST SAY NO

A police officer may legally request permission to search from any person who has the "apparent authority" over the vehicle (or over any container inside the vehicle). In

Robert Wilkins's case, the Maryland state trooper attempted to get consent from Robert's cousin, who was driving. *Granting permission to an officer means that you waive your Fourth Amendment rights—voluntarily.* Under federal law, police officers must ask for permission to search, and they don't need probable cause or reasonable suspicion to believe that the search would reveal evidence of a crime. But motorists must know that they have the right to refuse to give permission. Just say no. It's your constitutional right. (However, Peter Verniero's office noted that if a New Jersey state trooper has full probable cause to believe that a search would reveal evidence, he need not rely on the consent doctrine. He can proceed to initiate a search, even over the motorist's objection.)

New Jersey's standard operating procedure requires the person granting permission to sign a "consent to search" form. *Read it first,* because it spells out your right to refuse to give permission to search. If you're giving permission to conduct a search, you have the right to be present during the execution of the search and the absolute right to withdraw consent without giving any reason. If permission to search is withdrawn, the officer must immediately stop searching, unless he has already discovered evidence of a crime that would provide probable cause to believe that additional evidence is concealed in the vehicle. If this happens, the officer has the authority to continue the search. The justification no longer falls under the consent doctrine, but rather the "automobile exception" to the rules of issuing a warrant.

On initial contact with a police officer or state trooper, it is naturally considered that the driver of a vehicle has the "apparent authority" to consent to a search of the entire vehicle, including all of its contents. That is why the Maryland state trooper pressed Robert Wilkins's cousin to sign a "consent to search" form because he was the driver. However, depending on individual state laws, if a passenger asserts ownership over a given object (or the driver or other person granting consent denies ownership over a given object), the officer does not have the authority to search that object. Once again, the owner of that object has to sign a separate written consent form.

"STEP OUT OF THE CAR"

If a police officer has a legal justification during a routine traffic stop to conduct a frisk, it is a limited manual pat-down of the person's outer clothing, solely for weapons. If the officer detects an object that reasonably could be a weapon, the officer has the authority to reach into the clothes to remove the object. If the pat-down doesn't reveal an object that could reasonably be a weapon, the frisk is over and the officer has no authority to reach into the person's clothes. If the officer at this point did reach into the person's clothing, this would constitute a legal "search" and would require the officer to have probable cause. And if the officer had any reasonable suspicion to frisk anyone, he would also have the authority to order all passengers and driver out and conduct a limited "frisk" of the passenger compartment, but this limited inspection applies only to looking for weapons. If any drugs or contraband were found, they would be inadmissible in court. However, if at any point during the course of a routine traffic stop an officer observes or smells an item he immediately recognizes to be contraband or evidence of a crime, it is considered to be in "plain view," and the officer would at this point have probable cause to make an arrest.

What Robert Wilkins knew that very few young black men know is that when a family is driving home across interstate lines in the wee hours of the night, obeying the law, the family has the legal right to say no if they're pulled over and the officers want to search the car. If there is no probable cause, driver and passengers can refuse to give a consent to search. But that only means that in the suspicion of narcotics trafficking, drug-sniffing dogs will be called to the scene to examine the car's exterior. Federal courts consider this "minimally intrusive." It doesn't fall within the definition of "search" under the Fourth Amendment, since the dog can only react to illicit drugs and cannot reveal anything private about the car and its baggage. A search involving peeking, poking, or prying is a greater intrusion under the Fourth Amendment definition of privacy rights. It's also important that young minority (black, Hispanic, Latino, Asian, Native American, even young white) motorists know that any traffic stop that takes too long is considered a legal arrest in a court of law. Unless the officer has the higher legal standard of "probable cause," the lawfulness of a prolonged detention is generally questioned.

Should the police encounter end with the arrest of any or all of the car's occupants, they are then considered in state custody. They will be handcuffed, read their rights, and driven to the nearest state police station. The car and its contents will be seized as evidence, and the trooper begins the paperwork.

For a few minority motorists who are stopped for legitimate violations and are not racially profiled, the average traffic stop ends with a traffic summons or a written or oral warning. In both such instances most traffic stops take no longer than twenty minutes.

"THE AUTOMOBILE EXCEPTION"

1. You have the right to remain silent and refuse to answer questions. Do you understand?
2. Anything you do say may be used against you in a court of law. Do you understand?
3. You have the right to consult an attorney before speaking to the police and to have an attorney present during questioning now or in the future. Do you understand?
4. If you cannot afford an attorney, one will be appointed for you before any questioning if you wish. Do you understand?
5. If you decide to answer questions now without an attorney present you will still have the right to stop answering at any time until you talk to an attorney. Do you understand?
6. Knowing and understanding your rights as I have explained them to you, are you willing to answer my questions without an attorney present?

"You have the right to remain silent. You have the right to an attorney. If you can't afford one, a defense attorney will be appointed to you in a court of law. Anything you say can and will be used against you in a court of law."

Once a motorist is arrested, police officers are entitled to conduct a search of the person arrested and his personal space. The New Jersey Attorney General's office defines "personal space" to include the entire passenger compartment of the vehicle, including any closed containers therein that can be opened without causing damage to them. Troopers, however, cannot search the trunk. (Remember that individual state laws vary regarding what constitutes personal space.)

As previously mentioned, the federal courts will allow officers to search a passenger's closed personal handbag if they suspect that drugs are inside the car. An exception to the rules of a search-warrant requirement arises when police officers have probable cause to believe that a vehicle contains evidence of a crime and when there was no prior opportunity to have obtained a warrant. This "probable cause search" under the popularly known "automobile exception" does not limit the police to searching the passenger compartment; it extends throughout the vehicle to any place or container where there is probable cause to believe that the sought-after evidence might be concealed.

BIBLIOGRAPHY

- "Interim Report of the State Police Review Team Regarding Allegations of Racial Profiling," by New Jersey Attorney General Peter Verniero (New Jersey Department of Law and Public Safety, April 20, 1999).
- "Final Report of the State Police Review Team," by New Jersey Attorney General John J. Farmer, Jr. (New Jersey Department of Law and Public Safety, July 2, 1999).

CHAPTER 5

When Profiling Works

Terence K. Saulsby is the art director at *Black Enterprise* magazine. He's a young man, barely in his thirties, with a lot to say. His views are a bit unorthodox for a black man. His tastes are conservative, almost Republican, and very old school. Inside his Fifth Avenue office, classic Earth, Wind & Fire whispers from his computer speakers. Around him, his world is corporate—you know, suit and tie—professional and very rigid. And yet as odd as finding a black man marching in the St. Patrick's Day parade is finding a black man who doesn't see anything wrong with profiling.

Sitting with his eyes glued to the computer screen, making sure the magazine's layout is as close to perfect as it gets, with his back to the door, Terence shares the ideas that put racial profiling into his perspective. He says he's been stopped and profiled by police, security guards, and just ordinary citizens many times. Born and raised in central Florida, he has accepted profiling as an inevitable part of black life. Driving down the street in Florida in the normal flow of traffic doing nothing wrong, he said, could get you pulled over just because you were a black man with a certain look driving a decent car.

He suddenly swings around in his chair and throws his hands into the air, his smile wide. "Hold on!" he declares. "What we call racial profiling is not as bad as we make it out to be. A lot has been made of the term 'racial profiling' in the last five or six years, but cops from the dawn of time have always had criminal profiles, and people who meet that profile have always been targeted for searches. Right now we're focused on the 'racial thing.' But the police have criminal profiles that white people fall into, too. They get pulled over all the time, but we don't talk about it. You can't tell me that [white] cops in Arkansas don't see the longhaired, dirty-looking man in dingy jeans—who's half drunk and still drinking beer and riding around in a pickup truck—and say [to themselves], 'If I follow them long enough, they're going to do something wrong. And I bet they have drugs in the truck.' It happens to everybody; it's just not as nearly and intensely scrutinized as the 'racial thing' is. Now, what happens to people after they're pulled over, like police shootings and beatings—something that doesn't go on in the white community—that's another story. That's beyond my definition of racial profiling; that's about people who just don't belong on the police force."

Sound familiar? Former New Jersey State Trooper Superintendent Col. Carl Williams, months after he was fired, declared on a national television newsmagazine and in print that every law-enforcement agency and personnel profiles. It's only when you add in the racial component that it's wrong. Society wants to be drug-free, and in the course of achieving that goal, Williams said, it was perfectly fair for officers to scrutinize blacks. Williams had a thirty-five-year career as a state trooper, starting out as a patrol officer, then heading the narcotics bureau, ultimately becoming the superintendent of state troopers. He made previous "insensitive" remarks to the *Newark Star-Ledger*. He said this information is the same basic information that the President of the United States of America gets from his people. Williams publicly opined that the drug culture is controlled by minorities. In northeast New Jersey, Mexicans and Colombians control heroin traffic, the crack market is a black industry, and cocaine is controlled by people of Hispanic origin. He called I-95 a major artery in the distribution of drugs, and although he maintained that profiling would not be condoned whatsoever in his agency, the statistics said something else: 77 percent of the cars searched had blacks or Hispanics inside.

Terence leans back in his chair again, stretching. He chooses his words carefully, because he realizes he has ventured into controversial territory. An assistant designer silently steps into his office, allowing Terence to finish his thoughts.

He started off slowly. "Profiling is almost like a survival skill. Our experience has taught us that certain looks are of people who aren't doing the right thing. It's a profile. And I don't have any problems with that as long as it doesn't affect or harm anyone. But as for a police officer, or a security guard, or anyone else in authority, I would hope that he can look past his personal views. Unfortunately, a lot of cops can't do that, and they don't need to be on the police force.

"I'm looking at profiling on a more innate level. I'm up in the air about one particular notion: [If a report] says these are the things you look for—these are the signs—and if certain people meet certain criteria, and ninety-five percent of the time when a cop bursts them, they're going to find something—as bad as it sounds, I'm not necessarily opposed to that. But if the stats bear it out, then there's nothing you can do about it."

The idea has reached public debate. Police officers from around the country have gone on record saying that racial profiling is not racism at all. It's a tool—and officers have no intention of giving it up. In a nutshell, police officers in general consider themselves color-blind. But watch them on the job for several months and get them talking about the way policing is really done, and the truth will emerge that cops, white and black, profile.

Police officers have said they are justified in scrutinizing young African American males more closely than any other group because they commit a disproportionate number of street crimes. The justification is similar to that of personnel within the Los Angeles Police Department who handle the violent crimes being committed against people who sell jewelry. In most cases in California, Colombians were the predominant suspects. "We don't find Mexican-Americans or blacks or other immigrants," said the LAPD chief of police. "It's a collection of several hundred Colombians who commit this crime. If you see six in a car in front of the Jewelry Mart, and they're waiting and watching people with briefcases, should we play the percentages and follow them? It's common sense."

Police officers call racial profiling a very sensible, statistically based tool that enables them to focus their energies efficiently for the purpose of providing protection against crime to law-abiding citizens. And what about young white kids who get profiled? Randall Kennedy, the author of *Race, Crime, and the Law*, wrote in *The New Republic* that white people stick out in a suspiciously anomalous fashion (as potential drug customers or racist hooligans) when they are in a predominantly black neighborhood. In such cases, "their whiteness can become part of a profile." Police officers would consider this practice of racial profiling a very good piece of police work that proved to be an effective tool in fighting crime.

The *New York Times* printed some statistics that put the argument for racial profiling into perspective. "African Americans commit a disproportionate percent of the types of crimes that draw the attention of the police. Blacks make up 12 percent of the population, but accounted for 58 percent of all carjackings between 1992 and 1996. (Whites accounted for only 19 percent.) Victim surveys—and most victims of black crimes are black—indicate that blacks commit almost 50 percent of all robberies. Blacks and Hispanics are widely believed to be the blue-collar backbone of the country's heroin- and cocaine-distribution networks. Black males between the ages of 14 and 24 make up 1.1 percent of the country's population, yet commit more than 28 percent of its homicides. Reason, not racism, cops say, directs their attention."

Bobby Harris, deputy of the Los Angeles County Sheriff's Department, told Jeffrey Goldberg, author of the above, "Racial profiling is a tool we use, and don't let anyone say otherwise. Like up in the valley, I knew who all the crack sellers were—they look like Hispanics who should be cutting your lawn."

So what does a criminal look like? Young or old? A girl or a guy? One middle-aged Republican black woman I interviewed described her definition of a criminal as a black male in his late teens and early twenties, whom she always sees on her way home from work standing on a neighborhood street corner with his friends. Another black woman described any black man who is dirty, unkempt, and always asking for money on the street corner. A young white woman managed to describe an ordinary person with two arms, two legs, two eyes, a head, a nose, and a mouth who can be either black or white. Another woman described best what a criminal looks like: a man with a gun in his hands saying, " 'Give me your money.' He can be either black or white, Asian or Hispanic. All he needs is a brain and two feet to get away on." An anonymous cop on a New York City street corner said, "I've seen them come in all shapes, sizes, and colors. Nothing, and no one, surprises me anymore. You used to think of young punks committing crimes, now it's doctors, lawyers, bankers, and mothers who commit crimes. We all have the potential to be criminals. Why one person ends up a criminal and his brother doesn't is anybody's guess. I guess you need to be a psychiatrist to really understand it."

In essence, there isn't any one simple description of what a criminal looks like. If you put a group of people from any number of different cultures and races in a room together and ask them to describe what a criminal looks like, someone will describe another person in that room. People bring their own baggage to the task when they try to describe a criminal. One black woman I talked to who had been raped by a tall, French-speaking white man with short black hair, brown eyes, and glasses, described a criminal as a "tall, French-speaking white man with short black hair, brown eyes, and glasses." So why not a black man? Because she said she had never been the victim of a crime committed by a black man.

So where does the stereotype of the young black man as criminal come from? Television shows? News reports? The movies? Images flood into people's living rooms all the time of the young black man being hauled away in handcuffs. Do blacks have anything to do with this perception? Another person I talked to says yes. "Just look at rap music. You got these kids singing about walking up to someone and shooting them just because they come from another neighborhood. They make us frightened of them because of the way they portray themselves. If I walked around town with a gun in my hand talking about I'm going to start shooting black people because of whatever reason, black people would be scared of me too. It's all about the way I portray myself."

How does one young black writer who covered the hip-hop industry respond to that? "It's preposterous for society to think that. Rap music is show business. It's what they do to sell music. I believe the gangsta mentality is real on one level: Tupac Shakur and Notorious B.I.G. died gangsta style, and that was very real to me. But to a certain degree commercials have created an industry that is all showboat . . . a mad facade, and if society can't see past that, then they're cruising with their blinders on. Anyway, what does that rapper have to do with me? Just because Ice T is rapping about getting paid selling drugs and putting people who cross him to sleep [permanently], why does that mean white people have to follow me around in the stores? Or think just because I got loot in my pocket, it's crazy drug money? Ice T doesn't have anything to do with me, and I don't have anything to do with him. Where's the connection?"

We all have our own perceptions of what a criminal looks like, and descriptions are all relative. A young black woman I asked to describe what a criminal looks like had the best answer to date: "Hum, that's a good question. I don't know. I've never been mugged or robbed—let me knock on wood. I had a cousin who was robbed once, and the [robber] was black. But so was my cousin." When she was asked to describe the robber, she could only say, "It was so long ago, I forget what my cousin said he looked like. The only thing I know for sure was that the robber was a black man."

Any black man.

A middle-aged white woman I asked to describe what a criminal looks like paused, looked with hard eyes, sighed deeply, and chose her words carefully: "Let's see, I once went to Macy's to buy a coat and had my purse stolen. I sat my bag down on this bench in the section where the coats were, tried on a jacket, and I must have looked away for a few seconds. It couldn't have been more than twenty seconds. But when I went to get my things, my purse was gone. It happened that quickly."

Did she see any blacks nearby?

"No. I'm afraid not, not that I was looking for any. It was just a bunch of shop-crazed white folks trying to get through the madness of shopping for clothes."

Our point is to say racial profiling doesn't work. There isn't any one stamp that says, "This is what a criminal looks like." Although law-enforcement agencies around the country, including those of the federal government, have studies and statistics that say otherwise, in the end these statistics describe our own family members, our own cousins, our own neighbors.

Yet the argument contends that profiling does work. One officer told Goldberg in the *New York Times Magazine* article that "ninety-five percent of my drug arrests were dirt-ball-type whites. . . . Then I moved to the highway, I start taking off two, three kilograms of coke . . . black guys. Suddenly, I'm not the greatest trooper in the world. I'm a racist."

In an editorial published in *USA Today,* Dinesh D'Souza, a John M. Olin Scholar at the American Enterprise Institute and author of *The End of Racism,* wrote:

Far from being a myth, the reality is that young black males are, by far, the most violent group in U.S. society. Consequently, the treatment accorded young African American males by police officers, cabdrivers, storekeepers and others cannot be attributed to irrational prejudice. It is more likely the product of rational discrimination.

Insurance companies, for example, charge teenage boys higher car insurance rates than teenage girls (or older drivers, for that matter). The reason isn't sexism or anti-male prejudice; the statistical reality is that, on average, teenage boys are far more likely than teenage girls to bash their cars. So the insurance company is treating groups differently because they behave differently.

Profiling isn't limited to just the police. Little old ladies, black and white, do it all the time when they're walking down the street and they see a small posse of black boys. Back in Terence Saulsby's Fifth Avenue office, he continues his argument: "Like Chris Rock said, 'It's not the media who is scaring me; it's them brothers on the corner who are looking to knock me in my head. It wasn't Ted Koppel hanging outside my door a couple of nights ago trying to jimmy his way into my house, it was that [black guy] down there on the corner. . . .' It's a stereotype, and as wrong as it is, what I'm telling you is true. I'm trying to do the best I can: I got to keep my family safe. I got to keep myself safe."

But suddenly Terence raises a good question: "How much personal liberty do Americans give up in order to maintain law and order? The country is grappling with this question more and more. Certain people are willing to give up too much personal freedom because they think losing our freedom doesn't affect them. Some people in affluent neighborhoods are willing to say, 'Oh, yes, we don't have any problem with the police taking certain actions.' Why?" Terence asked. Because the police won't take certain actions, like profiling, against them.

"Sooner or later we all have to make a sacrifice in order to maintain law and order, to keep people under control," Terence explained. "That's something I'm willing to sacrifice, but I'm not sure how far I'm willing to take it. I don't have anything to hide, so if it takes searching my car, or searching every car cops come across that they think is suspect, then go ahead and do it."

Terence remembers a former roommate, a police officer who confessed that the vast majority of drug busts he had personally made arose out of car searches. It was an argument that convinced Terence profiling works, although he doesn't think that every time a black man is pulled over by a cop the motorist is being racially profiled. "If you're doing something wrong, and we all know you're wrong, whether you're walking or riding a bike, if you're doing wrong and a cop stops you and puts you through the works, and if the cop is doing his job, then I don't necessarily consider that to be racial profiling. We as blacks always jump on that: black man, white cop; it's got to be something else."

Terence says he's been pulled over and he's had his car searched "a number of times." He says he's never had a problem with it because he doesn't have anything to hide. "There is certainly a gray area—if I'm driving down the street minding my own business doing nothing that nobody else is doing, and a cop just happens to pull me over because I'm black and I fit the profile and he wants to search my car, rather than if I were doing something that made him get suspicious. Was it my color? Or was it my action? We usually dismiss the action and jump on the color thing, and sometimes we as black people just miss the boat. Same thing for a department store. Just because a security guard follows you around the store doesn't mean it's because you're black. It could simply be you fit the profile of someone who was trying to rob them the week before. Let's not make a big deal out of this color thing."

Terence speculates that blacks as a people in general go overboard too often. It's like crying wolf a few times too many when it comes to race and police brutality and being followed around in stores. "We know there is far too much police brutality out there, and too many store employees wanting to see more identification than is needed when purchasing expensive clothes, especially toward black people.

You never hear of a white person getting shot without a gun in his hands, or a white person being temporarily detained in a store because a clerk thought he was stealing something. But on the other hand, blacks can go too far."

Terence never thinks about becoming a victim of racial profiling when he gets behind the wheel of his car. He just hopes he doesn't get a speeding ticket. "Speeding is the only thing I do wrong. There is a lot to be said for an officer who handles himself correctly. I've been stopped by rednecks, and I've been stopped by guys who were only doing their job. I got stopped in South Carolina on the highway one night with some friends. I didn't know it at the time, but in South Carolina you have to pay your ticket right there on the side of the road or you go in and see the judge the next day. Tickets are like a hundred and something dollars, too. This particular cop said, 'You can pay me now or see the judge in the morning, and don't think he's going to see your black ass tomorrow.' "

Everyone wants to offer an answer to the problem of racial profiling, but no one has the one answer because there isn't one. There is no "This is the right way, and this is the wrong way" or "You people are wrong and we people are right." However, Dinesh D'Souza in his *USA Today* editorial makes a good observation: "Before we approve harsh punishments against those who practice racial discrimination, we should recall that their only offense is using common sense. Shouldn't African Americans who are legitimately outraged at being victimized by discrimination direct their anger not at cabdrivers or police officers, but at the black thieves, muggers and crack dealers who are giving the entire group a bad name?"

But is this fair?

I got no love for anybody breaking the law, I'm sorry. If you can't do it right, I don't have a problem with you being locked up. I'm not going to make excuses for everybody; however, don't just single us out, to put us in jail. If you put everybody in jail, I'm fine, but don't just come looking in my 'hood for criminals, because they're all over the spot.

—Terence K. Saulsby

BIBLIOGRAPHY

- *60 Minutes II,* CBS (October 19, 1999).
- "The Color of Suspicion," by Jeffrey Goldberg, *The New York Times Magazine* (June 20, 1999).
- *USA Today:* "Sometimes Discrimination Can Make Sense," by Dinesh D'Souza. Wednesday, June 2, 1999, page 15A.

CHAPTER 6

Riding the Train While Black

Black men get stopped by white officers, but black officers stop black women.—Amy Bowllan

my Bowllan took advantage of her midwinter recess from teaching social studies and science to fifth- through eighth-grade kids at New St. Brigid Catholic Grammar School on the Lower East Side of New York City by visiting her brother and his family down in Baltimore, Maryland, in 1997. She was twenty-nine years old that year and six months pregnant. Amy put on a pair of black pants, cowboy boots, her husband's black jacket, packed a duffel bag of other clothes, the tennis gear that she was returning to her brother, and, of course, her over-the-shoulder pocketbook and boarded a morning Amtrak out of Penn Station down to Baltimore. She passed the three-hour train ride reading a book on prenatal care.

Outside her window a beautiful morning slid past. Amy looked forward to seeing her brother and his five children in Randallstown. If she didn't visit then, seeing her brother would have to wait until after she'd given birth. This would be a minivacation for her.

The train pulled into the Baltimore station around one-thirty that afternoon. Of all the people who disembarked, most everyone was white, except for Amy and a handful of other black people. She dragged her gear out of the station so she could meet her brother by the taxi stand. He wasn't there, so she walked to the corner thinking that maybe her brother couldn't wait in the taxi stand.

When she saw the two black men approaching her from behind, she thought she was about to be robbed. They were dirty and unkempt. The man leading the approach looked like someone on crack—mid-thirties, thin, brown-skinned, partially bald, and wearing jeans, a sweatshirt and dirty sneakers. Bringing up the rear was his partner—very dark, very strongly built, and with very intimidating features. He hid behind a pair of dark sunglasses.

"Excuse me, ma'am," said the lead man. "I need to see your train ticket?"

"Excuse me?" Amy hesitated. A thousand thoughts ran through her mind.

"Where are you from? What kind of work do you do?" they prompted.

"I'm a teacher," she answered automatically. "We don't carry ID, but I have my passport."

By this point Amy had never been so scared. Her knees buckled at the thought of being dragged off the sidewalk, kidnapped, and possibly killed.

"Let me see it," the lead man said, glancing at his partner.

For a flicker of a second, Amy was shocked that the two men didn't attempt to steal her bag as she fumbled through it.

"Who are you? And why are you stopping me?"

"We work for the Baltimore Police Department," the lead man answered. He pulled out his badge. "I still want to see your train ticket."

"I need to see more than that."

The officer hesitated for a moment. He didn't expect that request. He pulled out his ID card with his name on it. But the request did nothing for the crowd eyeing Amy with suspicion. She was humiliated.

Making headlines that year in the region was the arrest of a black-and-Hispanic woman from Long Island who had been caught running a drug ring between New York City and Baltimore. Since the arrest, officers of the Baltimore Police Department had been detaining women who looked completely opposite the drug-courier profile—a sort of twisted reverse psychology.

"Let's go back inside the terminal."

"What are you carrying in your bags?"

They asked and she answered. She ran through the list of items she traveled with, including socks for her brother. Then suddenly she turned the tables again.

"Why are you stopping me? I just got off the train. I'm out here looking for my brother."

"Oh, are you really?" the first officer challenged. He insisted on knowing what else she had in her bags. "We check for drugs coming into the area out of New York."

As a former reporter and Emmy Award–winning journalist for a major television station, Amy knew the drug
stories all too well. "But you saw all those white people
getting off the train. Why did you just stop me?"

"We're just trying to get the heads-up."

"I don't have any drugs in my bags. You can open them
and see for yourself. But listen, I'm pregnant and I have to
use the bathroom. It was a long ride, and I didn't go on the
train."

"Sure," he said, "go on."

In retrospect, Amy figured it was because she walked
into the restroom for a few seconds and reemerged so
quickly that created a legal "reasonable, articulable suspicion." The officers snatched the opportunity.

"I'm going to have to search you, ma'am. You went in
and out of that bathroom too quickly."

"It was a nasty bathroom. It was crowded, and there
were no open stalls. Listen, I don't need this stress. I'm
pregnant."

"How do I know you're pregnant? You're probably stuff-
ing something in your clothes. How do we know you
didn't go in the bathroom and throw away your stash?"

"I didn't do anything. I just got nauseous inside there."

She handed over her bags to the muscular officer, who
didn't say much the whole time. Amy pulled out the socks
she was giving her brother, holding them as proof of her
word. She also pulled out her brother's tennis racket. They
even searched her lingerie.

Amy's humiliation intensified as people going in and
out of the restroom kept looking at them—kept looking at
her. And her, once a cadet for the New York City Police

Department! Amy figured that black women can't wear cowboy boots and that's why she was stopped; or perhaps they were just throwing their weight around. They would never do this to a white woman, she thought.

Amy's brother walked up on them. "What's going on?"

"They think I'm carrying drugs."

"There is a lot of drug traffic coming in from New York, and we're checking people, stopping it before it becomes a problem," the officer informed him.

"Why are you stopping my sister? She doesn't do drugs!"

"She looked suspicious because of all the bags."

"This is a tennis racket," Amy snapped. "What? A black person can't carry a tennis racket?"

"Well, you should have come for her on time. Then this wouldn't have happened," the other officer told Amy's brother.

"This is bull," he said. He took her bags and led Amy to the van out front.

Amy hasn't taken a train to Baltimore since this happened. And she vows, "I never, ever will."

Ironically, Jeffrey Goldberg reported in the June 20, 1999, *New York Times Magazine* that a black Baltimore police officer said that drug-interdiction teams operating at the city's train stations are looking for what they call the "Yo girls," young black women with long fingernails and hair weaves who carry Fendi bags. The officer told the *Times* that this is the profile of the people delivering drugs and money for dealers in New York.

"Of course we do racial profiling at the train station,"

the president of the Baltimore Fraternal Order of Police told the *New York Times*. "If twenty people get off the train and nineteen are white guys in suits and one is a black female, guess who gets followed? If racial profiling is intuition and experience, I guess we all racially profile."

In this case, Amy Bowllan was that one black woman who got off the train. But Amy proves the Baltimore officers wrong. Amy Bowllan doesn't have a hair weave, or long fingernails, or a Fendi bag. She was six months pregnant. She is as far removed from the "Yo girls" as she is from the planet Mars. She was stopped at the Baltimore train station only because she happened to be the only black woman getting off the train that day.

So don't believe what you read in the newspapers and magazines or what you see on television. These Baltimore officers are saying publicly that they're looking for a certain profile, but Amy didn't fit that profile and she was stopped anyway. The real problem with racial profiling is that people are stopped only because they're black. And that is the heart of the issue. If you are a black person, you have to be concerned that whether you fit a profile or not, there is a strong possibility of your being stopped. It can—and will—happen to you.

Amy's experience happened in the course of twenty minutes. And the fact that these were black officers proves that it isn't just white officers who racially profile, though they engage in the practice statistically more often. But as Amy would later explain, she believes that black officers can be worse than white officers, particularly when a black officer is trying to move up the departmental ladder.

"You don't see black officers arresting and harassing white citizens, but they want to make a statement by coming down hard on their own people," she said. "They all need cultural training. Not just the white officers, but the black ones, too."

Writing Letters: Tips from Amy Bowllan

When Amy returned home, she immediately started a letter-writing campaign. Although she had remained calm and let them search her bags when they had legal cause, Amy had turned the tables by requesting the police officer's identification. In her letters she included the names and badge numbers of both officers.

She wrote a letter to inform the sergeant of that particular precinct, the police commissioner, and the mayor of Baltimore that they must think twice before they stop another black woman who looks like her. She also followed up with more letters and phone calls to keep the matter from being swept under the carpet.

Amy's letter-writing campaign was successful. She received a warm letter of apology from everyone involved. However, the police officers at Amtrak never responded to her letters. As a result, she never rode that train again.

Tips for Writing a Good Letter

Picking up the pen is an old-fashioned way to make your point, and it works. You won't believe how much you can accomplish through the mail. It's an excellent way to create and track a paper trail. Making statements and complaints in writing gives your claim a tangible reality, the closest thing we have to setting something in stone.

Consider Amy's letter-writing campaign. In the end she got the apology she deserved and a letter of complaint against the two officers that will stay on their records as they journey through the ranks of the Baltimore Police Department. Some people have neither the time and money nor the energy to do legal battle through the judicial system. Victims like Robert Wilkins can afford to do so because they happen to be attorneys. But Amy, who was about to give birth to her first child, had to pick her battles carefully. This wasn't one she could fight in court, but it didn't mean she couldn't do anything. She could make enough noise from the comfort of her home so that people heard about it and apologized for it.

Complaint letters should always follow a basic format that is short, to the point, and above all professional.

- When at all possible, type up your letter in a standard business-letter format.
- Date the letter, address it to the appropriate depart-

ment, and whenever possible include specific names and official titles. You might have to make a few preliminary phone calls in search of the correct person to address a complaint to.

- If you do not have an exact name, address it to "To Whom It May Concern:".
- Carbon-copy (CC) and send the letter to other relevant people involved, including any third parties in a position to help you get action on your complaint.
- Briefly describe the incident, identifying everyone you remember, in the first paragraph. This is definitely the best place to name names. Don't be overly emotional, and don't go off the deep end with irrelevant information.
- In the next paragraph mention your suggestions for remedying the problem and express the redress you're seeking, whether it be an official apology or a promise that the guilty party will stop doing what you're complaining about. Ask for what you expect.
- Support your claim with relevant documents that chronologically detail your complaint. And never send original material; always make copies and send the copies. You will never get your original material back.
- Make clear that you are trying to remedy the problem peacefully. Include a daytime telephone number and an address so that the person you're writing will have the ability to respond.
- As politely as possible, demand a response by a specific date. Don't make threats, but explain that

you're expecting to hear from whomever you're complaining to and you won't let this just "go away."

- Always always sign the letter at the end.
- Put the letter, neatly folded, into an envelope. Address it with your return address on it, and make sure there's enough postage.
- If you choose to follow up the letter with a telephone call, wait until two weeks after the day that you mail the letter. This gives the letter time to get to its destination, time for a person to read it, and more than enough time for that person to take action. If you're following up with another letter, wait four to six weeks before doing so.
- Also allow four to six weeks for a response to your letter, which may be either a standard form letter or a personalized letter with more specific information.

The NAACP has been encouraging people to engage in a letter-writing campaign in support of the Traffic Stops Statistics Study Act. It would be extremely difficult for this book to provide examples of letters that respond to every incident of racial profiling. There isn't enough paper in the world for that. The oldest black organization in the country suggests you write regularly to your own congressperson or senator. Perhaps when enough people complain over the growing problem of racial profiling on our nation's highways, the practice will stop.

The following is a sample letter provided by the NAACP, which they suggest people, especially those who have been racially profiled on the highways, follow as a guide to writing their elected officials to complain about racial profiling and to support the Traffic Stops Statistics Study Act, which has been reintroduced to Capitol Hill once again this year:

[Date]
The Honorable [name of your representative/ senator]
U.S. House of Representatives/U.S. Senate
Washington, D.C. 20515/20510

Dear [name]:
I am writing to encourage you to actively support the Traffic Stops Statistics Study Act, which has been reintroduced time and again by Congressman John Conyers (D-MI) in the House of Representatives. This legislation, which is also known as the "driving while black" bill, passed the House with strong bipartisan support but was not acted on in the Senate prior to the latest adjournment. This legislation is important because it will require the Department of Justice to conduct a much-needed study of stops for routine traffic violations by law enforcement officers. The study would include consideration of several factors, such as identifying characteristics of the individual stopped, including the race and/or ethnicity as well as the approximate age of that individual, and whether a search was instituted as a result of that stop. The study would also look at

the number of arrests made as a result of these stops and searches.

Limited investigation suggests that 72 percent of all routine traffic stops occur with African American drivers, despite the fact that African Americans make up less than 15 percent of the driving population. A comprehensive study, such as the one that will be created with the passage of the Traffic Stop Statistics Study Act, would allow us to either support or dispute what is currently largely anecdotal evidence. This sensible and necessary legislation should be non-controversial, as it merely investigates the situation, and will provide us with the data necessary to determine if further action is warranted.

I hope that you share my support for this vital legislation, and that you will work with Congressman Conyers and others to see that it is one of the first pieces of legislation considered in the upcoming Congressional session. Please let me know what you intend to do to promote this legislation, and what I can do to help. Similar legislation has passed at various state levels, but we need the study conducted on a national, federal level.

Sincerely,

[sign and print your name, address and daytime telephone number]

It's important to know that when we're racially profiled, there are ways to retaliate. A letter-writing campaign is an honest start.

BIBLIOGRAPHY

- "The Color of Suspicion," by Jeffrey Goldberg, the *New York Times Magazine* (June 20, 1999).

CHAPTER 7

Shopping in a Group While Black

A COACH'S STORY

Howie Evans was the basketball coach for the University of Maryland at Eastern Shore in 1985. That year he and his team were on a three-game exhibition tour in South Carolina. When they arrived in Columbia on Thanksgiving Day for their second game, the team unpacked their bags, put on their warm-up uniforms, and stretched their legs. They were hungry from their travels. The National Urban League's local chapter had a planned Thanksgiving Day dinner for the basketball team, but until then they needed something to eat.

Normally, the coach wouldn't allow his players to roam around the city. It takes away the strength in their legs. But on this particular day he bent the rules. It was an exhibition game, so he let his team out. They picked a mall about a quarter of a mile from the hotel.

Evans immediately spotted trouble when the team stepped into the shopping mall. Two security guards who had been sitting nearby went into action. Evans didn't say anything to his team about the guards behind them, but he remained mindful. As the team meandered into the center of the mall, they split into little cliques. A few disappeared into clothing stores, another went into a music store, and a few more just window-shopped. Evans himself went into a Radio Shack to buy some batteries. He never expected to see the two guards placing six of his players against the wall.

"What's going on?" Evans asked as he walked up on the scene.

The taller guard, who had sergeant stripes sewn into his uniform, answered. "They stole something from one of the stores."

"What did you see them take?"

The sergeant paused to eyeball Evans. "Who are you?"

"I'm their coach," Evans answered. He pulled out his identification. "Did you see them take anything?"

"No," the sergeant answered, "but somebody told us they did."

"Show me who told you they saw my team steal something. I want to know what he saw."

"We can't do that. He's not here."

Antennas went up. "What? You're going to search these young men based on something somebody told you, and—by your own admission—he's not even here in the mall?"

"I'm doing my job."

Evans took a deep breath and chose his words carefully.

"You know, I watched you guys when we first came in here. You were sitting by the door, and when we got about fifty feet away from you, you got up and started following us. We've only been in here twenty minutes, and already you've accused us of stealing something. Why were you following us in the first place?"

The sergeant fumbled for an answer.

"I'm not going to let you search these kids out here in public," Evans continued confidently. "If you want to search them, you're going to have to take us down to the police station."

"I'll have to call them," the sergeant explained, almost as if he hoped the idea would make Evans stand down.

"So call them. If you don't, I will."

The sergeant detained the six players against the wall while Evans huddled with the rest of his team. Spectators watched from the wings.

"Look at these guys. What are they doing now?" a black woman whispered.

It broke Evans's heart that black people were walking away shaking their heads in embarrassment because they assumed that these young black men had done something wrong. The team promised him that no one had stolen anything and that it was all a setup. In fact, a black security guard was called to the scene—Evans now believes to justify that no one was being a racist—but after a few minutes of sizing up the situation, he threw his hands in the air in disgust.

"You guys are harassing them," the black guard said and walked away.

"We need you to stay here," the sergeant commanded.

"Give me a break."

But the sergeant wasn't hearing it.

While everyone waited for the police to arrive, Evans found a pay phone and called the local chapter of the NAACP. He explained his situation and asked them to send an attorney down to the scene. His second phone call was to the local black newspaper. He informed one of the editors of what was happening to his players. It was mere coincidence that a reporter for a local mainstream newspaper was in the mall at the time. Evans and the young reporter discussed everything.

In the meantime the sergeant let the six kids relax with the rest of the team, but he wanted everyone in a group.

"Don't panic," Evans told his team.

Evans suddenly saw the situation escalate into a potentially dangerous one. He had reasons to keep his team calm. Most of his players were young freshmen and sophomores who had never been on a collegiate road trip before. And for most of them this was their first time away from home on Thanksgiving.

On the other hand, the team was up against an out-and-out Southern racist with a gun. The sergeant stood about six feet and two hundred pounds, walking among the posse of the basketball players with an overbearing attitude and his hand continuously touching his gun. As Evans saw it, the sergeant was trying to impress the other guard by showing that he could take on these young black athletes, that he was someone who was used to grabbing black kids and throwing them up against the wall on a regular basis.

Evans kept a level head and remained very professional. He never raised his voice, just maintained a dignified degree of intelligence and poise. "Are you trying to intimidate us by walking around us with your hand on your gun? Don't you think that's dangerous?"

"I have the safety catch on," he answered.

"I would hope so," Evans said. "But doesn't that present a very intimidating presence, you walking around with your hand on your gun? These kids aren't going anywhere. They will move only if I tell them to move. If I told these kids to get up and run out, they would. But then you'd probably shoot one of them in the back. Right?"

A call blared over the walkie-talkie. The police were here. The sergeant met with the police and the manager of the mall, a man in his late twenties or early thirties, separately while Evans waited with his team.

Finally the manager walked over to Evans. "My guy said that they stole something."

"You know the only reason your guys stopped these kids was because they're black. Look at all these other kids in the mall; no one stopped them. These kids are college kids, and they're wearing identifying uniforms, so why would they go into a store and steal something with all this ID on? They don't even have pockets."

But the manager wasn't convinced.

"Your guy also didn't tell you that the person who told him these kids stole something isn't in the mall either. And your guy didn't see them steal anything."

The manager listened carefully, then walked away to confer with his team. "Stay here."

They took a long time.

"So what are you guys going to do?" Evans finally asked as he approached them. "You are accusing these guys of something simply based on who they are. As soon as my lawyer comes—I have an attorney on the way—we're willing to go to the police station, where you can search these kids. But if you search them here, I'm going to bring a lawsuit against you."

"You have a lawyer?" Everyone was surprised. "Just wait for us over there. We'll be there when we're done."

Evans remembers overhearing one of them calling him a wise guy and saying, "They always bring up this we-stopped-them-because-they-were-black stuff."

From a distance Evans could see that the police officers, who were also white, were concerned. "You guys had better handle this. We're leaving."

The policemen left before the NAACP attorney arrived. And as Evans filled in the details for the attorney, the sergeant's case seemed to crumble. Close to two hours after the team walked into the mall, the manager finally had little choice but to let them go.

"Perhaps you wouldn't have a problem, Coach, if you didn't have all these kids coming into the mall at the same time."

"What are you talking about? What am I supposed to do? Bring them in two at a time, go back and bring in two more? This is a team. Would you say that to anybody else? I think you owe us an apology."

"Don't get stressed, Coach," said the attorney from the NAACP. "They're always stopping our kids at this mall."

Neither Howie Evans nor his team ever received a formal apology from the city of Columbia, South Carolina, the manager of the mall, or the security agency hired to patrol it.

ARREST PEOPLE OF COLOR FIRST, THEN ASK QUESTIONS

Professor Charles Ogletree remembers the story of an artist who went to shop in a department store with an American Express card. He spent a couple of thousands of dollars in a very short time. He bought suits, clothes, a whole bunch of other items, and he signed his name. After he completed his shopping, one of the clerks who accepted his purchase got nervous and phoned the police. The police jumped the young man outside the store as he got into his car. They arrested him, brought him back into the store—brutalizing him in the process—and only after a few minutes of investigation discovered that he was the person whose name was on the credit card. When the clerk was asked by newspaper reporters the next day, after consulting with her bosses, why she had called the police, she answered, "Oh, it wasn't because he was black. That had nothing to do with it. It was because he was making some bad decisions in the things he was purchasing."

Professor Charles Ogletree is a professor at the Harvard School of Law and directs its Criminal Justice Institute. As the author of *Beyond the Rodney King Story,* a book relating to the NAACP's vision for policing the police, Ogletree is considered a leading authority in the world of legal issues regarding the police and its relationship to the minority community. He says "driving while black" was only the tip of the iceberg. Police misconduct goes deeper than racial profiling.

"As much as we talk about the drivers, there is also a crime called 'riding while black.' And for those of you who walk through the cities of New York, Washington, D.C., Los Angeles, Chicago, and Houston, there is a crime called 'walking while black.' And we don't see the books as much, but those of you who jog through Central Park, or Lincoln Park in Washington, D.C., or any park in Anywhere, USA, there is a crime called 'jogging while black.' There is also a nondiscriminatory crime that crosses gender lines called 'shopping while black.' You get all the tension in the world in department stores, so we all really have the phenomenon called 'living while black.' It's inevitable."

The sad element of the story above is that the police grabbed the young man without first checking to see if he really was the person who was signing the American Express transactions.

CAN SECURITY GUARDS STOP PEOPLE?

One New York City police officer I spoke with concerning the power of a security guard said a security guard has the power of a peace officer; a guard isn't allowed to carry a firearm, but as a part of his duties, if he sees someone shoplifting, he can stop and hold that person until a police officer arrives. Police officers call this a 1011, where security is holding someone in a commercial place. But let's take this a step further. The clerk who works the cash register, or the salesperson who is helping a customer, or even another customer who is just browsing has the same right to detain an individual as does a security guard. In cases where other citizens witness a crime in progress, any of those citizens can make a "civilian arrest" and detain the wrongdoer until a police officer arrives on the scene. In a civilian arrest, the good citizen has the right to physically restrain the bad citizen until an officer arrives. (But don't hurt anyone; the law gets tricky when someone is physically injured.)

So yes, security guards have the right to detain individuals, and they have the right to profile. Howard Amos, Jr., a part-time security guard who works various stadium security details like the Louisville Gardens in downtown Louisville, Kentucky, explained, "If there is an opera and everyone is dressed in formal clothing and all of a sudden someone walks in wearing overalls with a lit cigarette in his mouth, as a security guard I have the right to profile him, though it's not necessarily racial. And, as a security guard, I have the right to hold him or keep him from entering the opera. It's a security guard's job to watch the door to see who is coming and going into a show or a mall or a whatever is being guarded. If a guard believes a particular individual is coming into a particular guarded area to commit a crime or to do someone harm, the security guard has the right to hold a person in the name of security. That's how the police do it.

"Probable cause also applies to security guards. They are considered policemen without guns. Security guards are considered the 'judge on the scene.' However, if a guard asks someone to leave and the person challenges the guard's authority, then a police officer has to be called to the scene."

Take this hypothetical situation: Say a photographer sneaks his camera equipment into a Janet Jackson concert, and it's clearly posted that taking photographs during the show is not permitted. If a guard confronts the photographer, he might use the tone of his voice to assert his authority, but the guard cannot by law confiscate the photographer's equipment or film. If a challenge erupts, it is a wise idea for the photographer to request the presence of a police officer immediately. Again, a security guard does not have the right to confiscate personal property.

What to Do in a Similar Situation

Howie Evans thinks it's a good idea, if you're detained for "being black," to call the local branch of the NAACP and request an attorney's presence immediately. Only after you've secured the commitment of an attorney, then make it known that you have an attorney en route to the scene. Remain professional and calm. Don't get loud and start screaming in frustration.

As Evans explained, "Never permit yourself to be searched in the streets or in public. Whenever possible, request to be searched in the police station instead of going through the humiliation of being searched in the streets, or even in a department store or mall. Most people don't know they have that right."

Make a Call

Check your local listings for telephone numbers and addresses of organizations to which victims of racial profiling can turn. Some examples:

- National Association for the Advancement of Colored People's Legal Defense Fund
- National Urban League
- U.S. Department of Health and Human Services, Civil Rights Division
- District Attorney's office

When You Call the ACLU Hotline

If you believe you've been racially profiled, the ACLU invites you to call (877) 6-PROFILE. When you reach that number, you get a recording identifying the ACLU hotline. An operator will come on the line shortly to ask you a series of questions regarding your case.

A couple of days later you will receive a packet of information, including a thank-you letter, a driver's filing complaint form, a recent issue of the ACLU newsletter discussing racial profiling, a wallet-size card for easy reference regarding your rights when you're stopped by the police (rather on foot or in your car), and information about the ACLU Web site where you can file a complaint: www.aclu.org.

Reginald T. Shuford, a staff attorney at the ACLU in New York, handles complex cases involving constitutional litigation in the area of civil rights and civil liberties. He claims that the ACLU has done a lot nationally toward ending racial profiling. His latest case involves a black man and his twelve-year-old son who were stopped for two and a half hours and searched on the side of a hot Oklahoma highway. The officers had handcuffed the man to a trooper's car while questioning his son in the backseat of another car as drug dogs barked just inches away from the little boy's head. The officers took the man's car apart looking for drugs, and when they didn't find any, they released the two. When the father asked about putting his car back together, one of the troopers laughed and said, "We ain't good at repacking."

The ACLU for years has been in the forefront of the national education outreach campaign regarding profiling. The organization provided a national blueprint for pursuing litigation to be brought against police misconduct. As of July 1999, the ACLU has been involved in twelve "driving while black" cases in nine states: Maryland has three cases; New Jersey has one case (separate from Mr. Cochran's case of the four young black men shot at twelve times when their van rolled into a ditch); Indiana, one case; Pennsylvania, two cases; Illinois, one case; Florida, one case; Colorado, one case; Oklahoma, one case; and California, one case.

Tidbit

North Carolina became the first state to create a Traffic Stop Bureau in March 1999; Connecticut was

second, when the governor signed into law a similar
bill on June 28, 1999. Other states seriously consider-
ing passage of state laws requiring traffic-stop data-
collection units include California, Florida, Illinois,
Maryland, Massachusetts, Ohio, Pennsylvania, Texas,
Virginia, and Wisconsin. As of winter 2000, the governor of California vetoed a bill that had passed in the
General Assembly.

CHAPTER 8

Shopping Alone While Black

THE SILENT TREATMENT

The minute someone of color steps into a department store or an outlet mall or even a discount warehouse, there is the possibility that he (or she) will be racially profiled as a potential criminal, followed around by a security guard, scrutinized by a store clerk, or just plain ignored altogether by everyone. It doesn't happen to everybody all the time, but to minority consumers it happens often enough.

One day in 1999, the last order of business for Glenna Batiste, my wife and a mother of two, before she returned her rented minivan was to drive up to the Bronx to shop at a major carpet store in search of a sisal rug. It was a beautiful day in the middle of the week, and the store was relatively empty when she got there.

Stacks of carpets—Oriental, Persian, Turkish, Moroccan, small rugs, large rugs, heavy rugs, exotic rugs—were stored upstairs. Minutes passed inside the store before Glenna, who was browsing the second floor getting the lay of the land, so to speak, wondered why a salesman hadn't yet approached her with assistance. A white woman stepped onto the floor, and Glenna noticed a salesman immediately greet her.

Even when Glenna stumbled on a stack of interesting rugs, she still couldn't get help from someone who worked in the store. She tried to sift through the stacks of carpets herself, lifting them one at a time, but after about the fifth rug, they were just too heavy. Twenty minutes turned into forty, and her patience was wearing thin. A white couple stepped onto the floor, and again Glenna noticed another salesman approach them, guiding the couple through the inventory. When Glenna finally spotted someone, she walked up to him.

"Do you have carpets for children's rooms?" she asked.

The salesman barely glanced at her, pointing to the back of the store. "Yeah, there should be some back there." Without so much as a second thought, he walked away to help another woman—a white woman.

Close to an hour had passed since Glenna stepped into the store, and she still hadn't been helped. Suddenly it hit her: She could have spent another three hours at that store and no one would have helped her.

"Do you have to be white to get help around here?" she asked, abandoning the idea of buying a sisal rug at this store.

MEDIA EXPOSURE

Store managers, salesclerks, and even customers profile. Who knows why the salesmen at the carpet store ignored Glenna? No one from the store would respond. In fact, people in general don't want to talk about racial profiling. Whether from a person, a manager, a law-enforcement officer, or a co-worker, it seems that in order to get any insight into how and why racial profiling exists in department stores and outlet malls, you have to either pose as a private citizen engaging in off-the-record conversations with store clerks or go into a store with a hidden camera. *Dateline,* a national newsmagazine show, aired a hidden-camera investigation series entitled "The Color of Money" and "Under Scrutiny," exposing the racial discrimination and profiling that many blacks, like Glenna Batiste, experience on a daily basis. They showed America that two worlds exist for shoppers: one with a set of rules and store policies for whites and another with a set of rules and store policies (and employee attitudes) for blacks. In every case, people of color say, store rules and policies never work in favor of black shoppers. No one would admit to this publicly; that's why it took a hidden camera to expose it.

In "The Color of Money," *Dateline* asked this question: Do African American shoppers receive the same treatment as white shoppers? They sent two producers—a white woman and a black woman—out shopping at stores in New Jersey and New York City. Both women were about the same age and were asked to dress in roughly the same style. As a ground rule, the two women were to walk into each store around the same time, one just a few steps ahead of the other. *Dateline* admits that in some of the stores they visited, their black producer received fine treatment, but in a major department store on Fifth Avenue in Manhattan, the black woman received virtually the same type of treatment that Glenna Batiste received at the carpet store. While the white producer was greeted warmly by one clerk, who assisted her to her final purchase, the black producer had to wait for some time before someone helped her, and then she was passed off to another clerk. In another upscale store in New York City, a salesclerk let the black producer pass right by her before the clerk went to help the white producer. In fact, the black producer didn't receive service until after the white producer had left the store.

Even store policies concerning credit, merchandise returns and acceptance of personal checks change according to race. The same two producers were in a jewelry store, assigned to buy individual items that, they were told, could be returned for a full cash refund. When the black producer asked about the return policy on a pair of earrings, the clerk said that the policy was store credit or exchange only. No cash refund. With that said, the black producer left the store without buying anything. When the white producer asked about the return policy on a similar item, she was given the same information. But then the store clerk said he would talk to his manager. It was an unsolicited request. The clerk disappeared, and within a few minutes he returned to the second producer with an offer: She would have up to a week to return her item for a full cash refund.

Store Policies

In general you have the right to review the rules and policies of any store you want to do business with. You might take proactive steps like walking up to the register and requesting to see the store's policy in writing or calling the store beforehand and asking customer service to send you a copy; it is well worth the effort, especially if you expect trouble, received bad services in the past, or want to take legal action. Read through it, and once you understand it, begin your shopping. That way you know your rights in advance.

Also, many major franchise stores print a copy of store policy on the back of their receipts.

Filing a Complaint

There isn't much you as a consumer can look out for when you're being racially profiled, except to be aware of your surroundings. If a security guard is following you around the store, be aware of it. Note the time. The crowd inside the store. Was there something particularly odd that you were doing? Don't be confrontational; that doesn't solve anything. The same guidelines for how to behave if you're stopped by a law-enforcement officer apply to being stopped by security guards (see "What to Do When You're Stopped"). You might ask to speak to the manager, but verbal complaints have little legal weight should you decide to take legal action. Any and all complaints against any business—a retail store or outlet mall—are best made in writing. This way you leave a documented paper trail.

The American Civil Liberties Union, the organization spearheading the legal fight against racial profiling, can't handle every case of racial profiling presented to them. However, Reginald Shuford, the staff attorney and point man in the legal struggle, says that individual victims must bear the responsibility of taking proactive steps to fight their own individual battles whenever possible. And filing a complaint in writing is a great first step consumers can make themselves without the need of an attorney.

Although the Better Business Bureau doesn't handle complaints about employment practices and discrimination, the organization does offer excellent guidelines for filing a complaint against any business for any reason. The organization suggests you exhaust all of the procedures for filing a formal complaint as set forth by the particular company's policy before taking legal recourse. The Better Business Bureau, which handled over 1.3 million complaints against various companies in 1997, suggests that if you have a complaint against a particular business, you should do the following:

- Contact (in person or by telephone) a person in a position of authority at the business and as calmly and accurately as possible describe the problem and what action you would like the company to take to correct it. In all cases of profiling, the request should be to end its practice, sponsor diversity training among employees, hire more minorities at all levels of employment, and monitor how employees relate to minority consumers.

- Keep written records of all your efforts to resolve the problem. Note the names of the people you speak with, the dates, the time, and what was said.
- Save all documents you get from a store—e.g., sales receipts, repair orders, warranties, canceled checks, contracts, and any related letters to or from the company—in a single file. Organizing your papers is a must.

Should you decide to send a letter or an e-mail of complaint to a business, keep the following in mind:

- Type your letter.
- Address your letter to the president of the company.
- Include your name, address, daytime phone numbers, and account or claim numbers (if applicable).
- Make your letter brief and to the point.
- Include copies—do not send originals—of all documents that pertain to the company.
- Be reasonable, not angry or threatening, in your letter. Explain that the issue of racial profiling must be addressed among the business's employees.
- Keep a copy of your complaint letter, as well as copies of all letters to and from the company.
- You may want to send your letter by certified mail with a return receipt requested. It costs a little more, but it will provide proof that your letter was received and will tell you who signed for it.
- Send copies of your letter to your local and state

consumer protection office, your state attorney general's office, and the branch of the Better Business Bureau that services the area where the company is located.

Also, check your local listings for telephone numbers and addresses of organizations dedicated to fighting racial discrimination and profiling, including:

- Department of Consumer Affairs
- State's consumer-complaint department
- Department of Justice, Community Relations Services
- United States Attorney General, Civil Complaint Division
- Commission of Human Rights, Discrimination Complaints, bias hotline
- Local chapter of the National Association for the Advancement of Colored People
- Local chapter of the American Civil Liberties Union
- State district attorney's office
- An attorney who might be capable of representing you (if necessary)

Your state attorney general or local consumer-protection agency can help you find programs that resolve consumer disputes. If you have exhausted all procedures for filing a complaint and the company still hasn't resolved or even addressed your complaint to your satisfaction and you can't afford an attorney, you might decide to take the company into small-claims court. You don't have to be an attorney to initiate a case in small-claims court. However, it is always best at least to consult with someone who understands how small-claims courts work in your area.

For more information on filing complaints, contact the Consumer Information Center, Pueblo, Colorado 81009 for a free copy of the "Consumer's Resource Handbook," which offers tips on buying products and services. Also learn more about privately run programs by contacting the National Institute for Dispute Resolution at 1726 M. Street, N.W., Suite 500, Washington, D.C. 20036, (202) 466-4764.

You can file a complaint with the Federal Trade Commission by contacting the Consumer Response Center at (877) FTC-HELP (382-4357) or write to: Consumer Response Center, Federal Trade Commission, 600 Pennsylvania Avenue, NW, Washington, D.C. 20580. Ask for a complete list of publications on consumer rights.

For more information on filing a complaint with a particular company, visit the Web site of the Better Business Bureau at www.bbb.org/complaints/company.html. Or write for more detailed guidelines on lodging a civilian complaint yourself: Council of Better Business Bureaus, 4200 Wilson Boulevard, Suite 800, Arlington, VA 22203-1838. They offer sound advice even if they can't represent you in a racial-profiling complaint.

Guidelines for Writing a Complaint Letter

The Better Business Bureau offers this sample complaint letter as a guide for composing your own letter of complaint. Keep copies of your correspondence and once again never send original documents and materials, only copies.

Date
Name
Address
City, State Zip code

Name of contact person (if available)
Title (if available)
Company Name
Consumer Complaint Division (if you have no
    contact person)
City, State Zip code

Dear (Contact person):
(As briefly as possible in the first paragraph, describe the nature of the complaint and then describe the location of the store and the date you want to complain about. If you were followed by a security guard, state that you were and you wish to file a complaint.)

(In the second paragraph, explain that in order to resolve the problem, you would appreciate whatever specific action you want the store head-quarters to take to resolve the problem. In cases of racial profiling, refer to suggestions mentioned earlier in this chapter.)

(In the third paragraph, explain that you look forward to the company's reply and a resolu-tion to the problem. Mention that you will wait a set length of time before sending a follow-up letter. Refer to where the company can contact you.)

Sincerely,

Your name

Enclosure:
cc: Reference to whom you are sending a copy
of this letter

CHAPTER 9

Looking for
Air Jordan

Christopher Thomas remembers that Saturday in 1995 all too well. He had spent the day combing downtown Newark, New Jersey, looking for a pair of black-and-red, patent-leather Air Jordans. Air Jordans were hot that year, and every store he dropped into either had the shoes in the wrong size or had sold out just an hour before.

It was a lost day as far as he was concerned, so he turned around to head home, this time walking down a different street than he normally would take. It was strictly accidental that he stumbled on a small mom-and-pop shoe store with a pair of Air Jordans displayed in the window.

A Hispanic clerk from New York City greeted him inside the store.

"Do you have these shoes in a size ten?" Thomas asked.

"Definitely," the clerk answered and disappeared into the back of the store.

Thomas was feeling good; perhaps the day wasn't totally lost. He tried on the shoes and liked them. But understand Chris; he doesn't buy the first pair of anything he tries on. He's a meticulous shopper, knows what he wants, tries on different sizes, and decides what he likes by which fits the best. When he's playing basketball in the neighborhood, he likes his shoes to fit snugly.

"What about a ten and a half?" he asked. "You got them?"

"I'll be right back."

The clerk suddenly packed the Air Jordans away in the box and headed for the back.

"Wait a minute. Where're you going?"

"To get your shoes."

"Keep the tens out here. I just want to try on the ten-and-a-halfs to see if they fit."

"I can't do that."

"What do you mean you can't do that?" Thomas asked. "Just leave the shoes right here; they're not going any-where."

"If you want to see the tens again, I'll bring them back out."

"You mean you're going to take the tens back in the back, come out with the ten-and-a-halfs, and then go back there to get the tens again? That doesn't make any sense."

"It's store policy."

The clerk returned with the second pair. Thomas tried them on. "They're fine, but can you bring out the tens again?"

The subtleties of the incident had not yet sunk in. While the clerk was in the back retrieving the Air Jordans in a size ten, Thomas noticed a fortyish, stocky, dark-haired white man come from behind the counter that lined up against the long side wall and walk toward the door. On the other side of the store, another man meandered from within the women's section to the other side of the door. Thomas didn't think anything of it at first, but as he progressed to trying on the first pair of sneakers for the second time, he looked up and saw them standing by the door, almost expecting him to make a dash for it.

"What's going on with these losers in here?" Thomas asked the clerk.

"Man, they're like that in here. That's how they treat their black customers. They're crazy like that."

"They think I'm going to rush the door?"

"If I were you, man, I wouldn't even bother buying those shoes in here. They're funny like that with people like us. I'm telling you straight up, 'cause I'm outta here in a couple of weeks. I quit."

"You know how hard it was for me to find these?" Thomas asked.

"I wouldn't even sweat it."

Overall, Christopher Thomas is a calm young man who doesn't like to get into confrontations. He would admit that his only shortcoming is that he likes to shop for clothes because he likes to look good. Tall, lean, and well groomed, Thomas often dresses like a banker, in a blazer, slacks, and polished shoes, but today he had on a pair of casual jeans, a light jacket, and a T-shirt. To the outside world he was just another young black man in street clothes. Usually when he encounters racism, like being followed in an upscale store, he'll play with whoever is watching him. If he's treated right, he'll fold clothes back the way he picked them off the shelf, but if he's being watched and intimidated, he'll leave things out of whack.

Up until then it had been a nice day, but something about what was going on in the store that day just got him ill. He continued trying on his shoes, but simultaneously eyeing the two men at the door. He weighed the situation. On one hand a pair of hard-to-find Air Jordans and on the other a pair of racist store clerks—a dilemma he thought about for a moment.

On any other day Thomas would just have walked out of the store without saying a word. But the two men never bounced off the door.

"You know this isn't right," Thomas explained.

"Yo, man, tell it to the manager. He's right over there." The clerk pointed to one of the men standing at the door, the stocky one.

"You know, you're right," Thomas said after a moment's pause. "I'm not supporting this store. I'm not buying anything in this store."

Thomas walked up to the manager. "Ya'll could have made a sale today, but you blew it with your attitude. You're going to lose a lot of customers because of the way you treat people. You shouldn't be treating customers like they're going to steal something."

The manager was momentarily stunned when Christopher Thomas confronted him. And once the dam broke, he couldn't stop the rush.

"I'm in here trying to spend a hundred and ten, a hundred and thirty dollars, and you're going to make an issue about me trying on two pair of sneakers. What am I going to do, run off in a pair of your shoes? You think somebody wants to steal your shoes? I have a job. I have money. You could have made a killing here with me, but the way you act and treated me in here, I won't spend my money in your store."

This was the first time Thomas had ever encountered anything like this. He retaliated with a word-of-mouth boycott. He later told his friends about his experience at this store. In fact, a couple of years later, he and a friend were driving down the same street when his friend pulled up at the store.

"Remember when I told you about my experience in this store?" Thomas asked. "I told you about how they treat black people in there. They going to treat you the same way. How can you support that?"

"Oh, yeah," his friend answered. "I forgot."

Subtle Examples of Retail Profiling

- You walk into a store and immediately eyes greet you suspiciously. Trust your instinct. You're being profiled.

- A young man walks into a store wearing street clothes. There are other shoppers in the store. He wants someone to help him with an item, but no one shows up. Minutes later a white person walks in, and a clerk rushes to help the new customer. This happens all the time to young black men. It's a subtle form of racism.

- On the flip side, a young black customer walks into a store and picks up an item and immediately a clerk asks, "Can I help you?" "No, I'm just looking," the customer answers, and puts the item back. The clerk follows close behind, straightening up the item. If the clerk doesn't give the customer space to look at merchandise freely, the customer is being profiled.

- There are two stores belonging to the same chain in two different neighborhoods. The store in the upscale neighborhood doesn't make customers check their bags when customers walk in, but the store in the minority neighborhood does.

- A well-known rap artist was standing in line in an upscale department store when the woman behind the counter singled him out: "Young man, this line is for credit cards only." The rap artist was the only black person standing in the credit-card line. He had read the sign and had planned on purchasing his merchandise with his credit card.

Your Federal Rights Under Title VI of the Civil Rights Act of 1964

"No person in the United States shall, on the ground of race, color, or national origin, be excluded from participation in, be denied the benefits of, or be subjected to discrimination under any program or activity receiving Federal financial assistance."

To date, there are thirty federal agencies providing financial assistance via funds, training, or technical and other assistance to state and local governments and nonprofit and private organizations. Federally assisted programs address such broad and diverse areas as:

- elementary, secondary, and higher education

- health care, social services, and public welfare
- public transportation
- parks and recreation
- natural resources and the environment
- employment and job training
- housing and community development
- agriculture and nutrition
- **and, most important, law enforcement and the administration of justice**

There are many forms of illegal discrimination based on race, color, or national origin that can limit the opportunity of minorities to gain equal access to services and programs. Among other things, when operating a federally assisted program, a recipient cannot, on the basis of race, color, or national origin, either directly or through contractual means:

- deny program services, aids, or benefits
- provide a different service, aid, or benefit, or provide any of these in a manner different than that in which they are provided to others
- segregate or separately treat individuals in any matter related to the receipt of any service, aid, or benefit

Filing a Federal Discrimination Complaint

Each federal agency that provides financial assistance is responsible for investigating complaints of discrimination on the basis of race, color, or national origin in the use of its funds. If you believe that you or others protected by Title VI have been discriminated against, you should file a complaint with the federal agency funding that program.

A signed, written complaint should be filed with the appropriate federal agency, generally within 180 days of the date of the alleged discrimination. It should include the following:

- Your name, address, and telephone number. Your complaint must be signed. If you are filing on behalf of another person, also explain your relationship to that person (e.g., friend, attorney, parent, etc.).
- The name and address of the specific branch, office, institution, or department you believe discriminated against you.
- How, why, and when you believe you were racially profiled or discriminated against. Include as much background information as possible about the alleged acts of discrimination. Include names of individuals who you allege discriminated against you, if you know them.
- The names of any persons, if known, that the investigating agency could contact for additional information to support or clarify your allegations.

Once a complaint is filed, it will be reviewed by the agency to determine whether it has jurisdiction to investigate the issues you have raised. Each agency's procedures are different, but an agency generally will investigate your allegations and attempt to resolve violations it has found. If negotiations to correct a violation are unsuccessful, enforcement proceedings may be instituted.

The Department of Justice, under Executive Order 12250, coordinates the enforcement of Title VI and related statutes by all agencies that administer federally assisted programs.

If you cannot determine what federal agency may have Title VI jurisdiction, or if you do not know where to send your complaint, you may send it to the Department of Justice. As the governmentwide Title VI "clearinghouse," the Department of Justice will refer your complaint to the appropriate agency. The address is:

Coordination and Review Section
Civil Rights Division
United States Department of Justice
P.O. Box 66560
Washington, D.C. 20035-6560
(202) 307-2222 (voice); (202) 307-2678 (TDD)

Be aware that a recipient of a complaint charge is prohibited from retaliating against any person because he or she opposed an unlawful policy or practice, or made charges, testified, or participated in any complaint action under Title VI. If you believe that you have been retaliated against, you should immediately contact the federal agency with authority to investigate your complaint. This is often the Federal Bureau of Investigation.

HANDLING RACISM IN A DEPARTMENT STORE

Christopher Thomas knows that people of color spend billions of dollars on consumer products.

"So why should we allow ourselves to shop at a place that disrespects us?" he asked.

His approach to combating this problem was very basic. Economic boycotting, even by word of mouth, is a powerful, grassroots tool that proved effective in Birmingham, Alabama, during the civil-rights movement. And although his small boycott didn't have the same economic impact as a boycott by a whole movement of people, maybe one less dollar a day goes to that store based on his influence. Getting family and friends in the community to boycott a particular store sends a message about the little subtleties of economic power.

Tidbit

Did you know that New York State Congressman Adam Clayton Powell, Jr., was the first organizer of a bus boycott when he convinced the residents of Harlem, New York, not to use city buses because they refused to hire black drivers for the buses driving through Harlem, despite blacks' being the primary passengers.

It crippled the city bus system so badly that Dr. Martin Luther King, Jr., employed the same strategy when Rosa Parks was arrested for refusing to give up her front-row seat to a white man. And we know how that turned out.

Places to Turn To

Check local listings for telephone numbers and addresses of:
• Department of Consumer Affairs

- State Consumer Complaint Department
- Department of Justice, Community Relations Services
- United States Attorney General, Civil Complaint Division
- civil court, city small-claims court
- district attorney's office
- Commission of Human Rights, Discrimination Complaints, Bias Hotline
- National Association for the Advancement of Colored People, local chapter

LEGAL MANUALS AND INVESTIGATION PROCEDURES

In the fall of 1998 the Civil Rights Division of the Justice Department issued the "Title VI Legal Manual" and the "Investigation Procedures Manual" for enforcing the Title VI of the Civil Rights Act of 1964. The manual provides an overview of the legal principles governing Title VI. Its thirteen chapters identify methods by which federal agencies can evaluate and enforce compliance and obtain individual relief. Keep in mind that the legal manual isn't a complete, comprehensive directory of all cases or issues related to Title VI.

The "Investigation Procedures Manual for the Investigation and Resolution of Complaints Alleging Violations of Title VI and Other Nondiscrimination Statues" provides guidance on the investigation of discrimination complaints against recipients of federal financial assistance. In addition to focusing on the enforcement of Title VI laws, it provides information on all aspects of handling complaints, from initial receipt through resolution and monitoring. While it is designed primarily for investigating Title VI complaints, the investigation-procedures manual provides general guidelines that may be applied to investigating complaints of discrimination under other grant-related nondiscrimination statutes.

In general, the Department of Justice provides this material for both attorneys and laypeople in "user-friendly" language that acquaints them with situations to which Title VI applies, the types of discrimination the department prohibits, how to prove a violation, and how the statute is enforced by federally funded agencies.

BIBLIOGRAPHY

• U.S. Department of Justice, Civil Rights Division

CHAPTER 10

Flying While Black

WALKING THROUGH CUSTOMS

The tall black woman in the crocheted hat and her sister were two of the last people to disembark from the Air Jamaica flight. It was a late evening in April 1999. Yvette Bradley was returning home from a wonderful weeklong vacation that she'd given her sister as a belated birthday present. Once in Jamaica, they met up with a girlfriend who had brought over her mother, an aunt, and her sister. The vacation end up being an all-girls trip to a beautiful house set on a beautiful beach in Ocho Rios.

Now the vacation was over. It was Sunday night, and Yvette had to work the next morning. The flight had been fine. It was a little chilly in the cabin, so she stepped off the plane wearing her jacket and a favorite hat she and her boyfriend had bought on Valentine's Day. They'd purchased it the night she'd sung onstage in front of friends and strangers at an open-mike event, and she'd loved singing as much as she'd loved her hat, crocheted of tan, turquoise, and lavender yarn with pigtails that fell over her ears.

Going through the first checkpoint at U.S. Customs was simple. The agent inspected her passport and allowed her to continue to her luggage at the terminal's conveyor belt. Posted signs read NO RECORDERS. NO CAMERAS. NO CELLULAR PHONES IN THIS AREA.

"Man!" Yvette exclaimed. "We wouldn't be able to phone the outside world."

Another line up to the second checkpoint at U.S. Customs lay ahead of them, and there was no way around it. When the line split, the sisters separated, one into each line. Yvette thought that with any luck she and her sister would slide through Customs at the same time. In her previous travels she always considered herself lucky if she wasn't stopped at an international airport.

When Yvette stepped up to the counter, the agent silently studied her passport while Yvette silently studied the agent. He was white, maybe in his mid-forties, with cold eyes and a seeming chip on his shoulder. And that's when she noticed another line of mostly black women lining up for a secondary luggage search. Her instincts kicked into a fatalistic mode, and a voice in her mind seemed to whisper that she was going to be sent over there, too.

There were no computer terminals at this checkpoint to

tell the agent anything about Yvette. He could only look at her and her luggage and make a call, which he proceeded to do. He peeked inside her suitcase, closed it, and pointed to the secondary line. "Can you step over to line A?" he said.

Damn! Her sister had just stepped up to the counter in her line. With so many black people on the Air Jamaica flight, Yvette wondered why so many of them were being stopped and searched. Around her, white person after white person was being let through. A group of ten or so scruffy white college guys straight off spring break breezed right through without so much as a second glance.

"Come to my line," an agent demanded, singling Yvette out. He was in his late twenties or early thirties with light eyes.

"I should have worn a blond wig and blue contacts," Yvette said. "Maybe then I wouldn't have been stopped tonight."

But the agent just glared at her and proceeded to open her suitcase. "Was this your first time to Jamaica?"

"Yes."

"What were you doing there?"

"On vacation."

He paused and locked on to her, his eyes searching for something. "But what were you doing there?"

"I was on vacation."

"Well, what were you *doing* on vacation?"

"Doing vacation things."

"What were those things?"

Perhaps he wanted to see this woman dance and shuffle a little bit, but Yvette refused. As he pawed through each item in her suitcase, her backpack, and her purse, he continued to glare down at her. She'd had everything so neatly packed, but now this agent was tossing out all her personal items haphazardly. And left it all for Yvette to repack: reading material, bathing suits, T-shirts. She didn't have that much. After all, she hadn't gone there to spend money.

"I laid on the beach, I read, and I swam."

"But what else did you do?"

"I laid on the beach. I read. I swam."

"What kind of work do you do?"

"I'm an art director at an ad agency."

But he tried to look unimpressed and unconcerned.

"Where do you live?"

She sensed that this guy was intimidated by her success. He almost seemed to go out of his way to humiliate her and be rude. But when he went to the computer terminal at his station, she figured it was all but over. She took off her hat and started to reorganize her luggage.

"What's PHW?" he asked, handing Yvette her passport.

"Penthouse West. It's my apartment number."

She carefully placed her passport back into her purse and started to collect her luggage. Her sister had already gone through. They were out of sight of each other, so Yvette was eager to move on. Just as she started to walk off, the Customs agent stopped her.

"I need you to go to that door over there."

"Excuse me? What's going on?" she asked. "For what?"

"Just stand over there."

She threw down her purse beside her luggage and headed over to the door.

"You can take your purse."

She stopped and turned, a hint of frustrated anger slipping around her words. "No! You have violated me in every other way. I don't even want my purse." She walked off.

"No, not there!" the agent yelled. "Go to that door over there. Follow them."

Suddenly two female Customs officers (one white, one black) appeared out of nowhere and redirected Yvette to follow them.

"Where are you taking me?"

"Oh, no," complained the white agent, "not another one. I don't want to go through this again tonight."

Neither officer answered Yvette's questions. A wall of silence surrounded them until they walked her into a small, empty room with a metal table in the far corner. A few chairs were in place, but it definitely wasn't anyone's office.

"Take off your shoes," the agent instructed.

Yvette took them off, along with her jacket, as she was instructed. She was dressed in an ankle-length, lacy black dress that looked more like a slip.

"Go over there and stand against the wall."

In Yvette's opinion what had happened so far was uncalled for. Then came the unthinkable. U.S. Customs called it a routine pat-down, but Yvette Bradley claims that the white agent's hands lingered over her breasts and on her genitals. The hands never left her body, and she could feel the fabric of her undergarment being pushed inside her. She knew she was undergoing an invasive body search conducted by the United States government. She felt that she was being sexually assaulted and sexually violated. And it was all under the guise of a government search.

"I want to see whoever is in charge," Yvette demanded. "I don't believe this is happening."

When the white officer directed her to stand by the metal table, the black officer finally interrupted. "You know what? That's enough. We've seen enough. We don't need to do this tonight. You can go."

It took a second or two for this to register, but when it did, Yvette collected her jacket and walked out of the room. Her first request was to see a supervisor. "I want to file a complaint."

When she connected with the site supervisor, she lodged a formal complaint, which was sent to Washington that night. She requested a copy of the complaint, but the supervisor denied it to her.

"Next time," the supervisor said, "if you think something isn't going right, you should have asked to see the supervisor immediately."

An investigation later concluded that Yvette Bradley was stopped for a body search because smugglers use hats like the one she was wearing to import drugs. Yvette said the agents never asked to inspect her hat.

In Retrospect

- The moment you know that U.S. Customs agents are going to stop you, request to see a supervisor or site manager.
- Make sure the supervisor fills out a complaint form and mails it to Washington immediately.

CUSTOMS AGENTS UNDER
THE MICROSCOPE

The United States Customs Service told the House Ways and Means Committee's Subcommittee on Oversight that in 1998, the Customs Service seized more than 1,100 pounds of heroin and 3,750 pounds of cocaine as part of its Commercial Air Passenger operations. Customs officers are authorized to use strip searches, body-cavity searches, and X rays to detect smuggling by individuals who hide contraband, like illegal drugs, inside their clothing or who may swallow packets of drugs to smuggle in their digestive tract. Of the 71.5 million international-airline passengers who passed through Customs in 1998, 50,892 were subjected to some level of body search, most of them simple pat-downs. On a national level, 43.3 percent of those subjected to body searches that year were black and Hispanic.

Janneral Denson, an airline passenger from Fort Lauderdale, Florida, told Congress about her experience, which lasted from Valentine's Day through February 16 of 1997, while she was six months pregnant. About two o'clock on the afternoon of February 14, her flight from Jamaica arrived at Fort Lauderdale–Hollywood International Airport. Like Yvette, she had to pass through Customs. She got her passport stamped by the Customs agent at the counter, but as she was walking through the exit, another agent stopped her. They escorted her to a waiting room and searched her luggage. When the agents didn't find anything, they continued to harass her. They made Janneral Denson produce her birth certificate, proving she was born in Palm Beach County, Florida, her Social Security card, her husband's birth certificate, her wedding pictures—and when that wasn't enough, she was asked to write down her full name and address, where she worked, her phone number at work, and to describe her husband. When she requested to use the restroom, she was escorted there by two agents, who had her lean against the wall and spread her legs, and they searched her.

And still, Janneral Denson told Congress, that wasn't enough. The agents watched her use the bathroom. And because she'd been spotting, she always wore a panty liner. The Customs agents ordered her to show them the panty liner, as well as the tissue that she used to wipe herself after she had urinated.

Up until that point she had cooperated with the agents, but when she refused to cooperate any longer, one of them asked her to sign a legal paper. When Denson refused, the agent handcuffed her, put her in a van, and drove her to Jackson Memorial Hospital in Miami. By this point agents had taken away her personal belongings and denied her her right to call an attorney and her family. In the hospital, the doctor gave her an internal examination. Nurses took her blood pressure and a urine sample and handcuffed her to the bed rail. They also performed a sonogram, and all the doctors discovered was that she didn't have any drugs inside her.

You'd think that would be enough for them to release her from custody, but instead the agents placed her in a hospital ward, still handcuffed. The United States Customs Service, Denson told Congress, gave a pregnant woman a laxative and would not release her until she passed three clear stool samples. It wasn't until the next day that she was driven back to Fort Lauderdale Airport and released from custody. For the next two days she suffered from severe diarrhea and incredible pain. She told Congress that soon she began bleeding. Eight days later she was rushed to the hospital, where doctors performed an emergency cesarean. Her son, Jordan, was born weighing three pounds, four ounces. He was placed in prenatal intensive care for over a month.

> What I, and many other African Americans, have gone through points to a great failure in our country. Conduct such as this [that of the agents of the United States Customs Service] is both illegal and un-American and, in the long run, can only serve to drive a wedge between the government and the citizens of our country.
>
> —Janneral Denson, May 20, 1999

As of 1999, U.S. Customs faced a number of lawsuits over body searches, including a class-action suit by nearly ninety African American women alleging that they were singled out because of their sex and race. In 1997, Customs statistics showed that of all strip searches undertaken, broken down by race and gender, 46 percent of all searches were of black women. By comparison, white females were searched 23 percent of the time, and white males were searched 11 percent of the time.

Edward M. Fox, Esq., of Fox & Associates in Chicago, Illinois, who represents the class-action plaintiffs, says, "I have talked to many other women whose cases I didn't take on for various reasons, [like] the case is too old, or a case involved an airport other than O'Hare Airport in Chicago, and in none of these instances were drugs found."

The general scenario, as Mr. Fox reported to Congress, included women who were subjected to extreme personal searches conducted in this manner:

- They were questioned by a "rover," a Customs inspector who stands near the luggage area.
- After questioning, the women were made to go to a secondary area where their baggage was searched and further questioning performed. At this stage, gift bottles or bottles of wine are opened, and any kind of other gift destroyed.
- If an agent continued to have suspicion, the women were taken to a small, windowless room where agents conducted a pat-down search that often preceded a strip search and visual body-cavity search. Mr. Fox says that pat-down searches are typically conducted in an abusive manner.
- The women were generally asked, at this stage, if they are menstruating. However, they were searched regardless of the answer. Mr. Fox told Congress, "During a strip search, women have been subjected to everything from having hands inserted up under their clothes to being asked to take off all their clothes and underwear. In some cases, women were physically touched during the strip search and body-cavity search. In some cases, fingers were inserted into the body cavity of a woman."
- If a woman was taken to a hospital in handcuffs, that meant she was to be further examined and/or x-rayed. Telephone

calls were still not permitted at this stage, regardless of the length of time that had elapsed.

Keep in mind that when another step is made in this process, that means that no drugs were found, yet only a suspicion still exists. In the case *United States* v. *Montoya De Hernandez* 473 U.S. 531 (1985), the Supreme Court upheld a search in which at issue was the reasonableness of a lengthy detention in order to obtain a monitored bowel movement when the officers had only "reasonable suspicion" and not "probable cause" or a search warrant.

Who Is Being Searched?

Statistics presented to Congress indicated that black women are twice as often more likely to be searched than white women. Legislation is currently under congressional consideration that would require that travelers be given access to a lawyer within twenty-four hours of being detained, that a magistrate approve any detention beyond twelve hours, and that Customs inform travelers of both their rights and search processes and procedures. The agency would also be required to keep annual data on the race and sex of all passengers being stopped and searched.

Amanda Buritica also testified before the Subcommittee on Oversight on May 20, 1999. She is a Colombian-born United States Citizen who lives in Port Chester, New York. She told Congress that she was stopped at the San Francisco International Airport in 1994, strip-searched, and forced to drink a laxative because agents suspected her of carrying drugs from Hong Kong. She sued Customs Services because of the way she was treated and won a civil judgment of $450,000.

U.S. CUSTOMS COMMISSIONER SPEAKS OUT

Raymond W. Kelly, commissioner of the U.S. Customs Service, and his agency testified before Congress in 1999. Kelly said he is revising the Personal Search Handbook to require additional levels of approval and oversight from supervisors and managers for any searches. He is instituting a port-level, self-inspection and certification process. This means that port directors will be required to certify, in writing, that they are in charge of the personal-search process and that it is being carried out correctly at each individual port.

As expected, Kelly defended the Customs Service's policy with the position that "real or perceived, bias is not and will not be tolerated in any part of Customs operations. The drug cartels employ any and all means to thwart our interdiction activities, including smuggling drugs in the bodies of travelers arriving in our ports of entry. [In] 1998, Customs inspectors discovered over 1,100 pounds of heroin and cocaine smuggled [this way]. Finding these drugs is no easy task."

The commissioner noted that over 71 million commercial air passengers arrive in the United States each year. "Customs personnel must somehow sift the drug carriers among this vast number from the majority of law-abiding travelers. Smugglers, however, fit no single profile. They come in all shapes and sizes, social backgrounds and ethnic groups. Drug cartels will not hesitate to exploit anyone they can, especially those who would seem the least suspicious."

Kelly said that his agency will strive to improve personal-search procedures to ensure that the rights of travelers are protected at all times, and that this very special authority is used effectively, judiciously, and with minimal intrusiveness. Customs personnel work hard to carry out their jobs in a possibly difficult environment. In theory, it is a procedure that they undertake as a last resort and with the maximum of supervision. In practice, however, Kelly admitted that it is a procedure they have found in recent years to have suffered from insufficient training and a lack of supervision. Even Kelly added that this contributed significantly to the allegations of bias that surround the U.S. Customs Services.

"Our treatment of passengers undergoing the personal search has, in some instances, been sorely deficient. Communications with travelers detained for a search was poor, information was lacking, and legitimate questions went unanswered. We need to do a much better job of utilizing the interpersonal skills required for this difficult and delicate task."

For that reason, as of May 20, 1999, Kelly testified before the Subcommittee on Oversight that Customs has undertaken a variety of important measures to change its procedural policy (as opposed to the theoretical policy). The measures include forming an internal and external committee to review Customs' search procedures; immediate reforms to certain steps in the personal search, such as strengthening the role of supervisors; and far-reaching changes to Customs' passenger-processing environment that focus on improved information in training and technology. (In addition, the General Accounting Office [GAO] has been reviewing Customs air-passenger processing, and the GAO will provide an extensive report in May 2000.)

Here are some of the changes Customs has instituted:

- To make the personal search less intrusive, Customs now uses advanced body-scanning technology currently at JFK Airport in New York City and Miami International Airport. This technology minimizes the need for physical contact in a personal-search procedure. The device is used only at the consent of the traveler and permits inspectors to see if contraband is concealed under the clothing. Kelly said that plans are being implemented to install more of this technology in major airports across the country.

- Customs is currently developing a latex Breathalyzer, to detect whether passengers have swallowed drugs wrapped in rubber pellets, and mobile digital X-ray equipment. Used in combination, this technology reduces time spent transporting passengers to off-airport medical facilities for X rays. It also eliminates the need for restraint devices, like handcuffs, used during transport.

- All personnel will be better trained in order to minimize the poor treatment that some travelers have complained about. Customs inspectors are receiving additional training on developing their skills in interpersonal communications, cultural interaction, confrontation management, personal-search policy, and passenger-enforcement selections (that is, deciding who will be searched and who won't).

- New signs have been installed at major airports to better inform passengers about Customs' mission and how enforcement operations are conducted.

- Postage-paid comment cards will be prominently displayed at inspection-area exits to reach out to the traveling public by inviting passenger feedback. All correspondence, including these comment cards and general complaints, will be handled through the Customer Satisfaction Unit (CSU). It will be the duty of the CSU to ensure that complaints are correctly addressed and that passengers receive appropriate feedback, including a personal phone call to address their concerns. The CSU is responsible for keeping senior Customs managers informed on the concerns of the traveling public and for identifying any emerging trends on how they are delivering services.

- Passenger Service Representative programs will be designed to address passenger concerns in person, redefining the roles of individuals who are designated liaisons to the traveling public by having them spend more time on the floor and making them more visible to passengers.

- A center for passenger-enforcement data collection and analysis will keep accurate and informed data on all the personal searches filed by personnel agents. Customs inspectors must file comprehensive entries on any searches they conduct and report them to CSU.

- The Customs Declaration Form is also being revised to incorporate new information on the enforcement process.

- A new brochure better addresses the public on the most

frequently asked questions from passengers who have undergone an examination. Entitled "Why Did This Happen to Me?," the brochure is planned as an informational advertisement for in-flight magazines.

Customs takes the issue of personal searches and the recent controversy that has surrounded this authority very seriously. We will continue to do whatever we can to improve this process, and to work with Congress to ensure that the dignity and rights of all individuals are protected as we carry out our mission.

—Raymond W. Kelly, Commissioner,
U.S. Customs Service

Did You Know?

The following information comes compliments of Robert M. Tobias, president of the National Treasury Employees Union (NTEU), which represents approximately 155,000 federal employees, about 13,000 of whom work for the Customs Service.

Customs Mission
It is the mission of Customs inspectors to stop drugs from coming across the United States borders. They are devoted to eradicating the drug use in the United States.

Customs Inspectors
Customs inspectors present the first line of defense to the illegal importation of drugs and contraband across our borders at the sea, land, and air ports. In the

course of their daily responsibilities, they have been assaulted by travelers, shot at, dragged to their death or near-death by cars running the ports, threatened, and accosted. One Customs inspector in Puerto Rico was shot on his way home from work simply because he was recognized as a Customs enforcement official.

Customs inspectors have both demanding and dangerous jobs. They carry weapons and undergo mandatory firearms training. They are taught to make arrests. They learn defensive tactics for protecting themselves from dangerous criminals with whom they may come face to face. They learn to be courteous but at all times on guard and wary of the traveler who may present a danger to the Customs inspector or to other travelers. The ordinary travelers don't recognize inspectors, and most inspectors work a minimum of three different shifts with odd start and stop times. They have little control over their schedules, and they are constantly on call to work overtime.

The average salary base for an inspector, even after twenty-four years of dedication, is about $40,000 a year. Unlike their counterparts in the DEA, FBI, and Border Patrol, Customs inspectors do not have law-enforcement status.

Traffic Increases
Customs estimated that over 470 million land, sea, and air passengers walked through American ports in 1999, up about 10 million from 1998, and up 23 million from 1997.

Processing Travelers

Inspectors usually don't know the people they encounter in the course of their duties. Sometimes they receive advance information about arriving passengers, but generally they don't. It's up to the Passenger Analysis Unit (PAU) to determine how to handle day-to-day operations, and usually there are too few PAU employees to properly analyze the data and provide it to the inspectors. They generally don't have enough staffing to field the necessary number of "rovers" who walk among the passengers and watch for odd behavior and actions.

In addition to staffing shortages, according to the president of the NTEU, there is a "profound lack" of technology and information-gathering equipment to process travelers adequately. In most cases a passenger will be cleared immediately after retrieving his or her luggage. In others, Customs inspectors might ask several questions. Far less frequently inspectors will direct a traveler to the secondary area for a personal search. Mr. Tobias says that most ports of entry allow for only 2 percent of passengers to be reviewed in the secondary area.

Profiling

"There is no typical drug smuggler or a typical way to smuggle drugs," says Mr. Tobias. "Heroin has been strapped to human couriers, sewn into the lining of a traveler's jacket, compressed into the soles of a traveler's hollowed-out tennis shoes, poured into condoms and ingested, and hidden in luggage or any other type of belonging. Smugglers and distributors are teenagers, college graduates, middle-aged business people, senior citizens, and young children. They are single, married, traveling with babies, in a tour group, or alone. Customs inspectors must be attentive in their efforts to detect who is carrying drugs and how. Of course, drugs are not in plain view. Some smugglers have hidden drugs so well that they may evade body-scanners deployed in [today's] airport terminal."

Tobias claims that the most effective method available to Customs inspectors in their search for concealed drugs is the personal search. "In 1998, Customs seized over 2.5 tons of illegal narcotics on and in the bodies of drug smugglers. Any invasive physical contact is unpleasant for a traveler, and while less intrusive methods of searching the bodies of suspected smugglers are available, these body-scan machines are extremely expensive and have been deployed in Customs areas in just two major airports so far."

POLICIES AND PROCEDURES ON PERSONAL SEARCHES

According to Tobias, the national president of the National Treasury Employees Union, whenever a passenger is referred to the secondary area for a personal search, an inspector must follow the Customs Service's nationwide policies and procedures. Inspectors at every port of entry around the country are taught these procedures when they receive their initial training at the Federal Law Enforcement Training Center. But these policies must be frequently reiterated and relearned so that inspectors who may not perform personal searches regularly are aware of every nuance, change in policy, or added procedure. To date Customs doesn't provide standardized update training to continue the education process and alert inspectors to new patterns and methods of smuggling. There is no follow-up training after inspectors have been working for several years, in which they can comment on the policies and procedures, and Customs can reinforce their understanding of the law and policies on personal searches. There must be regular, formal training opportunities for Customs enforcement personnel.

Zeroing In on the Target

Customs inspectors do use criteria developed by the Customs Service through the analysis of historical data that help to narrow the field between the innocent traveler and the drug smuggler. It's as close to racial profiling as Mr. Tobias gets. Indicators like the traveler's origination of flight, including whether the traveler's flight included a stopover in a source country, the duration of stay, the method of payment for the ticket, the traveler's employment history and many other details help agents determine who to stop and question. Most indicators come out during a quick interview with an arriving passenger. In theory, the interview process narrows a search to those who may be attempting to smuggle drugs. Just how high the agency's current rate of accuracy is, is currently (as of summer 1999) under review by the Independent Personal Search Review Commission as chaired by the Honorable Constance Berry Newman, Undersecretary, Smithsonian Institution.

CHAPTER 11

Living While Black

WHAT TO DO WHEN YOU'RE STOPPED

Clifton Hollingsworth, Jr., remembers one night in the tenth grade when he and a classmate were aboard a parked school bus waiting to return home following a basketball game. He and his friend found empty seats in the back of the bus, over the engine, and, with the game still in their minds, rehashed the excitement. They weren't on the bus five minutes or so when suddenly sirens and flashing lights sliced through the night. Clifton and his friend paid little attention to the sirens since they hadn't done anything wrong, nor to the unfamiliar white man getting on the bus and approaching them.

"Shut the fuck up!" the white man said.

"What?" Clifton said, gesturing, when suddenly he felt the cold steel barrel of a gun pressed against his temple. In a matter of seconds he was escorted off the bus to an await-ing unmarked police car parked behind it. In the backseat sat a white woman.

"That's not him," she said.

The plainclothesman tapped Clifton on the back and said, "Go ahead. Get back on the bus."

Thirty years ago Clifton had no one to talk to about the incident. He told his parents about it, but they felt they had no legal recourse. It was a different world then. No one on the bus took offense to what had happened to Clifton. In today's community-action environment, people would have been outraged enough to be sure it made the five-o'clock news. But back then no one came to Clifton's aid. No one interfered with the police. No one got excited about a gun being pointed at a black boy's head.

To this day, New York City Detective Clifton Hol-lingsworth, Jr., doesn't know who the officers were, what they looked like, or why they pulled a black teenager off his school bus at gunpoint.

Eric Josey, a black New York City police officer and a member of One Hundred Blacks in Law Enforcement Who Care (an organization based in New York), wants the average young minority individual to know that racial pro-filing does exist, has always existed, and will continue to be a national problem.

In the Big Apple, the Street Crimes Unit—the branch of law enforcement responsible for shooting Amadou Diallo, hitting him with nineteen of the forty-one bullets they fired—stopped over twenty thousand residents during 1997 and 1998. Of that number, said Howard Safir, the city's police commissioner, not one was arrested for drugs or guns. Yet Mr. Safir claimed that overall crime was down.

And the Street Crimes Unit saw a 50-percent reduction in civilian complaints over the previous two years. In addition, NYPD as a whole has had an 11-percent drop in civilian complaints over the same two years.

Safir makes sure the numbers look good for his department. But Officer Josey, like Detective Hollingsworth, knows that there are many people out there who accept police stops as a given and realize that to complain about them doesn't really solve anything. This is why officers like Josey and Hollingsworth and the crew at One Hundred Blacks in Law Enforcement go around to various communities sponsoring workshops that show today's minority youth "what to do when stopped by the cops." Bronx District Attorney Robert Johnson, the first black elected to that position in New York, visited one of those workshops at Rice High School in Harlem. Students learn through various role-playing exercise how to behave when stopped. Though most workshops might be aimed at young people, the principles can be applied to anyone of any age of any ethnic background.

Racial profiling is a tool that police departments across the country have used for years. However, when anyone claims that it is an effective tool for officers to use, Detective Hollingsworth will strongly disagree. He has three sons, so for years he's been sensitive to the issue of racial profiling. He knows as a detective assigned to Brooklyn, New York, at the turn of the millennium that law enforcement can do its job very effectively without racially profiling.

"It's all too easy to prey on the minority community, those who may or may not know their civil rights and the laws that govern them. Naturally, it's easy to use and abuse the people who don't have a voice. As long as those in power allow it to continue as a tool that law enforcers use, it will be used against you and me, and it will also be used against our children, and our children's children.

"When the police violate someone's civil rights merely because of the color of his skin, then the officer is profiling because of race, and it makes the officer racist toward certain groups of people. Anytime he sees a black or Latin male or female, the officer is naturally going to see that person in a different light than if he had seen anyone else of any other ethnic group."

Born and raised in the Bronx, Detective Hollingsworth knows about racial profiling. He, like many blacks, has been profiled often. It happens—and will happen—to most young black people who live in the inner city. Hollingsworth has been with the NYPD for over seventeen years, and he knows that young black men and women are going to be stopped primarily because of their skin color, their race, because of the area they happen to be in at the time, the clothes they're wearing, the vehicles they're driving, or the time of day or night. These are all factors of racial profiling.

PATROLLING THE STREETS

The white New York City police officer works the overnight shift at the 77th Precinct in Brooklyn. The people he profiles are out at four in the morning looking to buy drugs. This isn't racial profiling; he calls it good police work. What criminal behavior stands out in his mind? He says that when he drives around the Crown Heights and

Bed-Stuy sections of Brooklyn in the early mornings and he sees the same people standing on the same corners when it's twenty or thirty degrees, they stand out. He said when he drives around the block three or four times and those same people are still there, there is a basis for reasonable suspicion. When he's detaining people in a car or on the sidewalks, he's always polite, but too many times people give him attitude. From his perspective, these people don't realize the power he has behind a shield and a gun. All the officer wants is a little respect. His routine is simple. He detains people, asks for their paperwork, tells them what they did wrong, and gives them the benefit of the doubt to explain themselves. If a person has a legitimate answer, the officer uses his discretion either to give a verbal warning or issue a ticket or summons.

A law-enforcement officer pulls over your car and asks for your license and registration. You show that officer your documents. Suddenly he tells you to step out of the car. He wants to search you and your vehicle. You ask him why. If the officer can't explain why, then consider your rights violated.

"Can I look in the trunk?" he asks.

"Let me look in the glove compartment," he says.

"Let's see under your seats," he demands.

This type of police encounter is experienced by young people of color on a daily basis in New York City, for no other reason than it happens to be a weekend, or it's late at night. Racial profiling is four black men in a car at night, and police officers decide to pull them over because they "looked suspicious." They interrogate them, order them out of the car, search all the men and the car for no reason other than that they were four black men in a car driving late at night.

Detective Hollingsworth explains, however, that if an officer *can* explain himself, the situation is different. And although it's a young black man's right to say no to any search, Hollingsworth suggests you keep in mind that to exercise that right raises the level of suspicion and creates more conflict and friction. If an officer commands you to step out of a vehicle and you say no, he is within his rights to drag you out, and if you make the slightest physical contact with him, he can arrest you for assaulting an officer. And that's a felony.

Anytime you walk into a racially profiled situation where you're confronted by a man with a gun, especially a police officer, you need to know how to "deescalate" the situation and "survive the moment" so that you can take appropriate action by filing a complaint or initiating civil litigation against the officer, his or her department, and the city.

"Never get into a verbal confrontation late at night, when no one is around," says Hollingsworth. "Never! Comply with the officer. If it means getting down on the ground, then get down on the ground. Comply with whatever the officer is asking you to do. Don't let the ego get in the way. An ego can get you killed. You can always fight it on another level. The real way to beat the officer is to file a complaint against him. It's within everyone's right. Everyone should know how and where to file a complaint."

Detective Hollingsworth explains that it is the way you conduct yourself when you're stopped by the police that makes the difference between going to jail, going home, and going to the morgue. Each time you are stopped by a police officer, your life hangs in the balance. When you create problems, the officer will treat you badly. The best tactic is to remain calm. Say something like "Officer, I don't really understand. Could you explain to me what's going on?" Naturally, coming from a police perspective, Detective Hollingsworth suggests you let the officers search whatever they want to search. If they see that you aren't posturing, or showing off, or being disrespectful, they will treat you better. They may still go through your pockets or toss you around, but at least you'll survive. Creating an opportunity for constructive dialogue allows you to go home, tell your parents, and engage your community leaders. If they have you down on the ground with their guns drawn, then *definitely* comply. Listen closely to the officer's instructions, and don't make any sudden movements—don't go for your wallet, don't reach for a cell phone, don't do anything but put your hands up in the air. If you notice other people around watching, speak up loudly so that they can hear, and don't be aggressive. Be polite and show that you're complying, so that you have witnesses on your side. Draw an audience. People who are quiet during a police encounter often create a perception among pedestrian witnesses that they're guilty.

At the same time, don't question the officer or tip your hand about future plans to file a complaint. Remember, uniformed officers have their names pinned to their uniforms across their chest, and plainclothesmen must show their shield. And there's nothing wrong with asking questions. But if an officer tells you to shut up, don't talk. Hollingsworth says, "It's asking a lot, but he has his reasons.

Give up a little self-pride and 'survive the moment' so you can live to file a formal complaint. Otherwise, if you're loud and filled with so much pride that you won't be disrespected, then know that you will end up going through the criminal-justice system. On average that includes three days in a holding pen and thousands of dollars to get you out of a felony charge, or whatever charge they pressed on you, just to show the world you have rights."

That isn't recommended. Surviving the situation means enduring the encounter and making a complaint against anyone who has violated your civil rights. Know that your civil rights are violated when you tell an officer, "I don't want you to go through my pockets," and he does anyway. Also remember that the officer must fill out a 250 form if he searches you. Otherwise, it's a violation. If policemen knock on your door and you tell them that they can't come in, but they burst down your door anyway, without a warrant, your civil rights have been violated. You might be tempted to say, "Well, they're going to cover it up and say I did something," but don't believe that. You never know what you can accomplish until you try. Your case just might be the case. Officer Josey admits that in the past more often than not in the black community, a young man has been complaining that his civil rights have been violated because he's been stopped, confronted, and frisked, but when he initiates a complaint, it went unheard. Rather true or not, today if your rights have been violated you must complain through official procedures.

It is vitally important that the victim be capable of identifying the officer through his shield, or his name badge, and by taking certain identifying action so that when the encounter is over, and the victim knows that his civil and constitutional rights have been violated, he or she can take appropriate action.

Josey says, "We recommend that you don't verbally ask for his shield number—more than likely an officer in uniform will have his number displayed—and also because that only escalates the situation. You take mental note of it." Whenever possible, say the officer's name if you see it. Let him know that you know his name. If everything goes smoothly, there is no reason to complain.

Official Imprints

As a matter of policy, every time a police officer stops someone, he is required to fill out a police form that makes an official record (or imprint) of that stop. The form details the name of the person being stopped, where the person was stopped, and what the "legal predicate" was that allowed the officer to make that stop. The form remains on file at the police department so that there is no secrecy about any stop made by any police officer.

Keep in Mind

Racial profiling as a matter of public policy is illegal, despite a 1996 Supreme Court decision that allowed police officers to stop cars for traffic violations, even if the purpose is, say, solely to search for weapons and drugs. One Hundred Blacks in Law Enforcement Who Care travel throughout New York, New Jersey, and Connecticut sponsoring workshops to help young people understand how to behave when stopped by the police. One of their most important messages, says Lt. Eric Adams, a New York City police officer and founder of the organization, is that people can empower themselves to deescalate certain police encounters. When stopped in a car by the police, he suggests that you:

- turn on your interior dome light
- put your hands on the steering wheel
- take note of the time and date
- always let them see your hands
- listen to the officer
- don't reach for an item without first telling the officer what you're reaching for
- don't place your hands in your pockets

It's attention to these little details that could save your life.

If You're Stopped

Know your civil rights. When a police officer asks to search your car, know that it is within your rights to refuse. Very politely say, "I would like to exercise my right to say, 'No, I don't want my car to be searched.' "

- **Don't argue.** If you refuse to let them search you, the police will try to detain you on the roadside. You may ask, "Am I free to leave now?" It is unwise, however, to be contentious or confrontational.
- **Take names.** If you believe police officers have violated your rights, as soon as you're able to get hold of a pencil and paper, write down names, badge num-

bers, license-plate numbers, and any details that you remember regarding the encounter.

- **Take action.** You can file a complaint against the police, or you can sue in a civil court. Talk to an attorney or your local office of the NAACP or ACLU. Also, contact the Citizens Opposing Profiled Police Stops (COPPS) at (757) 624-6620 or visit its Web site at www.copps.org.

Keep in Mind

Your behavior means everything.
- Stay calm and relaxed.
- Carry identification at all times.
- Never run. You can get shot running away from the police.
- Better to walk away from a police encounter with a bruised ego than a bruised body. So don't try to win.
- When the police encounter is over, move on to contacting the proper people to file a complaint against the officer who violated your civil rights.
- Never go to the same precinct that violated your rights to fill out a complaint form. They do have the ability to cover up the incident. Detective Hollingsworth suggests you go to another precinct for the form or contact Internal Affairs. Write down all of the details that you remember. If the police precinct gives you a form and you're unable to fill it out, an officer is required to fill it out for you. When it's completed, the officer will read it back to you and have you sign it. If you're not

comfortable with that idea, take the form to a local politician or minister and have him fill it out for you. Be sure to sign it.

- If you're a minor, inform your parents when your rights have been violated.

Did You Know?

- In 1993 there were 212 NYPD shootings; in 1998 the number of shootings went down to 112.

An Observation

Detective Hollingsworth says that in a seminar he conducts entitled "What to Do When Stopped by the Police," anytime he asks children over fourteen years of age if *they* have been stopped, many hands go up. "It's a way of life," he said. "Blacks have accepted the fact that it happens all the time."

Consider This

An officer might be just as scared as you are when he approaches you. A lot of officers overcompensate for that fear with a strong tone or harsh voice in an effort to take command of the situation. Why do they do it then? Well, a fireman is also scared every time he approaches a fire, but he still has to perform his job. The point is to remember they come across so strongly because they are scared.

THE POWER OF GOOD POLICE WORK

Racial profiling is never positive. Good detective work is good police work. Observation is good. If a police officer observes a person do something, and he locks him up for that, or searches him for those reasons, then that is good police work. But stopping someone for nothing more than the color of his skin is bad police work. There will never be a time when racial profiling in police work, or any other work, is positive. When an officer observes a series of strangers go up to a young man, and they disappear inside a building for fifteen minutes or so and then come out, though he's never witnessed any exchange of drugs and money, the behavior creates a suspicious belief that gives officers like Hollingsworth the "probable cause" needed to go up to that person and ask questions.

"What are you doing?"

"Do you have ID?"

"Let me see your ID."

And if the answers to the officer's questions lead the officer to believe there is something else happening, or that the person has something on him, then the officer has the protection of New York laws to stop and frisk the person, as long as the officer can articulate in a court of law why he stopped the person, questioned him, didn't like the answers the person was giving, and frisked him. Articulating that the officer was concerned for his safety is equally valid.

In this scenario, this police encounter isn't racial profiling. From the officer's point of view, it is an officer doing good detective work. He observed the individual for fifteen to twenty minutes engaging in what the officer believed was suspicious activity. Profiling is when a police officer stops and searches a luxury car merely because a young brother with dreadlocks is driving it.

THE NATURE OF PROBABLE CAUSE

Probable cause means that a law-enforcement officer has a reasonable belief that a crime is being or has been committed by a specific person. If that person is you, this means that a witness has identified you, or a victim has described you as a suspect, or an officer has observed your suspicious behavior.

Regardless of whether an officer has a search warrant or not, protect your rights by making it clear that you do not want to be searched and you have done nothing illegal to warrant a search. If a search is conducted anyway, never resist. The police are within their rights to conduct a pat-down search of your outer clothing for weapons.

LEVEL OF SUSPICION

The problem with the Amadou Diallo incident was that the four officers didn't allow the situation to play itself out in a peaceful manner. They did prejudge Mr. Diallo, seeing a black man in the Bronx, late at night. And even if the world gave the officers the benefit of the doubt—even if he were the Bronx serial rapist the officers were looking for—the officers didn't allow the situation to develop in a positive manner.

They came out with their guns drawn, prejudging him, thinking they were stopping the man who was wanted for a series of criminal rapes. That level of suspicion didn't afford the officers the opportunity to take steps to protect themselves and Amadou Diallo.

The first steps the officers should have taken was to radio in a description of the man who was going into a certain address. They should have called in to the precinct for backup. Even if Mr. Diallo had been the rapist, and he went into the building, how difficult could it have been for a large police department like New York City's to surround the building and flush him out? The officers took that situation and reacted, instead of merely observing. And whenever you're in a "reactive mood" in any situation, you're not going to handle it very well.

WHAT DETECTIVE HOLLINGSWORTH TELLS HIS SONS

It's nice for your child to be fashionable. But realize as parents that clothes are mass-produced. The chances of two people wearing the same designer clothes are high. If your son has on the same shirt as a man who just robbed a store, then odds are that your son will be pulled over or stopped.

It's important for any person to have his own individual style and quality. Don't try to fit in with the latest styles, because those styles may cause you to be arrested and misidentified. It happens all the time. It's easy to misidentify a dark-skinned male wearing a red coat. Detective Hollingsworth doesn't let his sons wear their caps backward or their pants hanging down below their waists. He makes his sons stand erect. Parents, you need to check your children.

Reinforce to your child that life is precious. Parents need to instill in their children that they are to look, act, and carry themselves in a certain way. When in Rome, do as the Romans do, and in American society it's important that families do as much as they can to help prevent their children from getting stopped, frisked, and killed by police officers.

Detective Hollingsworth remembers a white officer who observed a black kid constantly adjusting his pants because they were too baggy. The officer used the constant adjustments as a "probable cause" to approach the young man. Hollingsworth specifically remembers the officer saying that if he didn't like the young man's answer, he was going to search him.

"I believe the young man has a gun," the officer had said.

In essence, today's children have to be conscious of the signals they send to other people, including police officers. At one time, for example, police officers in New York City were looking for young people wearing gang colors. And it would be within the officer's right to approach anyone wearing colors to see if they're drinking beer or shooting dice. They profile you, because they're looking for something.

Just as the adults in our community tell our children to say no to drugs, or to wear a condom when having sex, we also need to tell our children what to do and how to behave when they're stopped by the police. These are the small things that can save our children's lives. As responsible adults, it's our personal responsibility to give that lesson to our children, because if we don't, we're telling the cops, "Hey, they're yours. If you think you have probable cause to shoot my child, then do so; probable cause to arrest my child, then arrest him; probable cause to beat my child, then do so, because we didn't train him well enough." When we train our children how to behave when they're stopped by the police, we are providing them with tools they'll need to survive.

As a black officer who understands the inner workings of the police department and the streets of New York, Detective Hollingsworth knows that certain police ways will not change.

"If we wait for that change, then we wait a lifetime. The best we can do is to tell our community leaders to help us teach our children."

The real way to beat an officer is to handle the situation. Look the officer straight in the eyes, look at his badge number, at the name tag that he wears on his uniform, and smile. Address the officer by name. Don't give him a hard time, and let him know that you don't deserve to be disrespected. In the long run, know what you need to do. Know whom you need to call. Know where you need to go to get the necessary complaint forms. But never tip your hand; don't tell the police what you're going to do. Don't tell them that you're going to launch a complaint. They'll find out soon enough, from their supervisor.

What the ACLU Recommends

The American Civil Liberties Union had been investigating racial profiling for years before they published their report in 1999. Although there are very few original ideas anymore, they do make a point that with regard to your rights and the police you always think carefully about what you tell the police. What you say to the police is important. As the Miranda warning explains, what you say can and will be used against you in a court of law, and it can give a police officer an excuse to arrest you. It is within your rights not to answer a police officer's questions, but you must show your driver's license, registration, and proof of insurance when stopped while driving a car. In all other police encounters, you cannot be legally arrested for refusing to identify yourself to a police officer.

If a police officer says he has a warrant to search you, your house, your car, or any other personal property, ask to see it. And read it carefully. Take your time. Do not rush through it. Otherwise, if he doesn't have a warrant, you do not have to give your consent to the officer to search you, your car or your house. If you choose to give your consent, it can affect your legal standing later in court. You can always recede your consent.

But as the ACLU suggests, never interfere with police officers performing their duties, even if they search you illegally. They can arrest you for it. Instead, file a complaint later. The ACLU also suggests that if you are stopped by the police to:

- **Remain silent.** You do not have to answer any questions and you do not have to show them any identification unless you are operating a car or are in a place where liquor is sold or served. However, both the ACLU and this book suggest that during any police encounter you provide the basic information of a photo identification that shows your name, address, and date of birth.
- **Never run from a police officer.** If you are placed under arrest, always ask on what charges. If you are not under arrest, you are theoretically only temporarily detained and should be free to leave within a reasonable time. The courts have held that if a temporary detention is prolonged, it is legally considered an arrest.
- **Never physically resist an officer.** The police may frisk you for weapons by patting the outside of your clothing. They cannot search through your pockets or ask you to take off your shirt. However, make it clear that you do not want to be searched. If they search you anyway, do not resist. Comply. But file a formal complaint later.
- **And listen to the officer.** Listen carefully, because each word from an officer carries legal weight and repercussions.

There is no substitute for getting an understanding of your legal rights by consulting with an attorney. This book recommends that you make an appointment with an attorney to consult how local highway laws apply to your state. Naturally, what is illegal in one state might not be necessarily illegal in another state. However, if you are arrested for any reason, the following is only a basic listing of items to keep in mind:

- Submit to being arrested. It's inevitable that you go through some sort of central booking center en route to the criminal-justice system. The best advice is to learn from the experience. You have twenty-four hours to contemplate whatever charges got you into the filthy bowels of a holding pen.

- You have the right to remain silent. Exercise that right. Never explain yourself with stories and excuses and why you shouldn't be arrested. Just tell them your name, age, and place of residence.

- Call your family or your attorney immediately. The police will make you wait a half hour or so, but they have to accommodate your request. If you can't afford a lawyer, wait until you appear in court and get to speak with a court-appointed attorney. Never talk to the police until your attorney is present.

- Whether or not the police obtained a search warrant, ask to see it. Insist that you do not consent or agree to any searches. In any case, don't physically resist.

- The police are required to provide you with a receipt for everything they've confiscated during their search, including your wallet (and its contents), your watch, your jewelry, any packages or bags that you were carrying when you were arrested. When you're released, you can return to the station that processed you to collect your personal items.

- You must appear before a judge the next court day to be released with or without bail or held until further notice. Exercise this right, and request to see a court-appointed attorney if you are not being represented.
- Never make any decisions regarding your case until you have consulted an attorney.

The Overview

In general, it's best for all people of color to know what the police can and cannot do and how best to behave when you encounter a police officer. It's best to take a moment to contact your local representative to find out what laws are on the books in your state. In the wake of the New Jersey Turnpike racial-profiling cases that dominated the news during the late 1990s, many state legislatures have passed or adopted laws governing police procedures, statistical collection, and basic overall reforms. Your local political representative will best be in the position to help you learn the new laws affecting you.

To sum up what we've covered in Part One of this book, police officers must have a "reasonable suspicion" to believe you are engaged in criminal activity or have information regarding any criminal activities in order to stop you. As the ACLU recommends, you have the right to ask why you're being stopped. If the police officer doesn't answer you and you believe you were stopped for no cause, file a complaint at a later time. And don't tell the officer of your plans. Remember, if you're driving a car, you must show identification. However, any other time you have the right to remain silent. You do not have to answer any questions, including telling your name, your age, and your address.

If you are detained for a significant amount of time, the courts have held that to be a legal arrest. There are three types of arrest: misdemeanor, felony (both of which are criminal arrests), and civil. Misdemeanor arrests usually include minor traffic offenses and minor assault charges. If drugs are involved, it's usually in small quantities. However, felony arrests carry long prison sentences and include serious violent crimes and aggravated assaults, rapes, and burglaries. If drugs are involved, it's usually in large quantities.

Then there is the civil arrest, which doesn't include any criminal behavior. Men who are arrested for not paying their child support are considered to have been arrested under civil jurisdiction, not criminal. This means when you're taken to a detention center, you are placed into a separate holding cell, apart from the holding cell where criminals are held. If you are under the age of eighteen and you are taken into police custody, they must take you to a juvenile-detention center, separate from the detention center where they keep adult offenders and suspects. If they process you through the criminal-justice system, they are also not allowed to take your photograph.

Generally in the past, an officer would read you your Miranda rights at the point of arrest. However, it is only required that you be informed of your rights prior to any police interrogation. Your Miranda warnings are as follows:

1. You have the right to remain silent and refuse to answer questions. Do you understand?
2. Anything you do say may be used against you in a court of law. Do you understand?
3. You have the right to consult an attorney before speaking to the police and to have an attorney present during questioning now or in the future. Do you understand?
4. If you cannot afford an attorney, one will be appointed for you before any questioning if you wish. Do you understand?
5. If you decide to answer questions now without an attorney present you will still have the right to stop answering at any time until you talk to an attorney. Do you understand?
6. Knowing and understanding your rights as I have explained them to you, are you willing to answer my questions without an attorney present?

Keep in Mind

If an officer uses excessive force, a suspect has the right to defend himself. Just keep in mind that resisting will only make the situation worse. When police officers believe that a suspect is being argumentative and confrontational, the need to subdue the suspect's behavior rises, many times to the point of calling for police backup. If you happened to witness an officer behaving wrongly during an arrest, never try to interfere. Instead, pay attention to the details of the event so that you can testify for the suspect/defendant in a court of law. Note names and badge numbers and ask other witnesses for their names and phone numbers so that they, too, can be witnesses.

Report the incident to your local politician, to your local community leaders, to Internal Affairs at the city's police department, and to any (and all) civil-rights organizations, including:

- the ACLU
- the National Urban League
- the NAACP
- the U.S. Department of Justice
- the Federal Bureau of Investigation
- the United Stations Survey of Crime Trends
- Amnesty International
- and your local attorney general's office.

INSIDE YOUR HOME

The ACLU publishes a small traveler's card that contains relevant information about what you should do if a police officer knocks on your door. Here's what they suggest:

- If the police knock and ask to enter your home, you don't have to admit them unless they have a search warrant signed by a judge.

- However, in some emergency situations (when a person is screaming for help inside, for example, or when the police are chasing someone) officers are allowed to enter and search your home without a warrant. If the police say they have a search warrant, ask to see it, and read it.
- If you are arrested, the police can search you and the area close by. If you are in a building, "close by" usually means just the room you are in. Don't interrupt or interfere with the police; you can be arrested.

IF YOU ARE STOPPED ON THE STREET FOR QUESTIONING

The ACLU also wants you to keep in mind the following:

- It's not a crime to refuse to answer questions, but refusing to answer can make the police suspicious about you. You can't be arrested merely for refusing to identify yourself on the street.
- Police may "pat down" your clothing if they suspect a concealed weapon. Don't physically resist, but make it clear that you don't consent to any further search.
- Ask if you are under arrest. If you are, you have a right to know why.
- Don't bad-mouth the police officer or run away, even if you believe that what is happening is unreasonable. It could lead to your arrest.

BIBLIOGRAPHY

- *Public Material* copyright © 1996–98 ACLU-Washington.

Part
Two

CHAPTER 12

Anonymous Poetry and Government Legislation

When you look at me: What do you see?
Am I not innocent until proven guilty?
Why must I be your enemy? You were hired to protect me!
—anonymous poem left on the doorstep
where Amadou Diallo was killed,
as provided by U.S. Senator Charles E. Schumer

n the wake of the Amadou Diallo shooting in New York (the African immigrant shot forty-one times in the vestibule of his building by four police officers in the Street Crimes Unit operating in the Bronx), incoming U.S. Senator Charles E. Schumer (D-NY) delivered his first speech on the floor of the Senate chamber on March 25, 1999, informing the United States Senate that blacks and minority groups in general, and those in New York City in particular, are frustrated over the widening racial rift between minorities and police departments. Senator Schumer explained that while New York City has enjoyed a tremendous drop in crime, that drop doesn't give police officers the right to hassle and humiliate people. Since the four officers of the Street Crimes Unit opened fired on the unarmed African immigrant a month before, New York City—like New Jersey—was thrust into the national spotlight.

Schumer told the Senate that the model behavior of many officers doesn't undo the fact that black men and women (particularly in New York City and Los Angeles) are all too often made to feel like lawbreakers. A resident of Brooklyn, New York, Senator Schumer is surrounded by the black community. And throughout his campaign to unseat longtime incumbent Senator Alfonse D'Amato, Schumer heard informal complaints from members of local churches and on the streets about law-abiding people who've been stopped, frisked, and harassed by police officers for no other reason than the color of their skin.

"And they know this doesn't happen to white people. They know white people are treated differently."

But having absolutely no reason to fear law enforcement is the difference between being a person of color and being an average white person. Senator Schumer is white. To his people, he says, widespread frisking and patting-down is a small price to pay for the steep reduction in crime that New York City experienced in 1998 and 1999. "But most white people have never been frisked and have no conception of how pervasive the practice is. But talk to a black stockbroker on Wall Street or a black lawyer downtown, people who wear a suit and tie every day; that person has a story of being stopped, frisked, and harassed by a cop.

"If you take the time to listen, the views of minorities about the relationship they want to have with police can be summed up in five words: 'protect me and respect me,' " Schumer told the Senate. "Whatever facts emerge from the killing of Amadou Diallo, or for that matter the killing of a

Syracuse man, Johnny Gammage by the Pittsburgh police [see chapter "The American Civil Liberties Union Report"]— whether it's guilty, not guilty, suspension or removal—our society must deal with the underlying problem of race and law enforcement." (This he told the Senate in 1999, more than 30 years after the beginnings of the black civil-rights movement, more than 130 years after the Emancipation Proclamation, and 223 years after the Declaration of Independence. As long as two or more races exists on the same land, racial issues will exist.)

It's extremely dangerous when law enforcement is based on racial and ethnic stereotypes and physical characteristics that a person cannot change or control; it's also extremely dangerous when law enforcement agents don't follow the known method of procedure for objectively observing a suspect's behavior. This causes members of the minority community to live in fear of being detained or stopped simply because of their skin color. And this is a national problem. Peter Verniero's "Interim Report" documented that other states along Interstate 95 had similar arrest statistics for minority motorists because they all got the same stereotypical information from the same source, the Drug Enforcement Agency. Operation Pipeline is a prime example of misinformation being distributed to individual agencies that result in a national problem.

Unfortunately, only states can regulate themselves. A few state troopers have checked themselves. Up until the mid-1990s, police departments didn't keep track of whom they pulled over according to class, age, race, or dress. A few police chiefs, however, surprised the minority community. In San Diego, Chief Jerry Sanders ordered his department to start tracking and making regular public reports of traffic

stops, including the race of the motorists. In North Carolina, the state legislature passed a bill requiring an official
study of North Carolina Highway Patrol traffic stops.

The Traffic Stops Statistics Act of 1999, as introduced on a
federal level by U.S. Representative John Conyers (D–MI) and
co-sponsored by New Jersey Congressman Robert Menen-
dez, would mandate that the U.S. Attorney General's office,
through appropriate means, acquire data about all stops for
routine traffic violations by law-enforcement officers.

Included in this data would be information pertaining to:

- the number of individuals stopped for routine traffic violations
- identifying characteristics of the individual stopped,
  including the race and or ethnicity as well as the approximate age of that individual
- the traffic infraction alleged to have been committed that
  led to the stop
- whether a search was instituted as a result of the stop
- how the search was instituted
- the rationale for the search
- whether any contraband was discovered in the course of
  the search
- the nature of such contraband
- whether any warning or citation was issued as a result of
  the stop
- whether an arrest was made as a result of either the stop
  or the search

The NAACP Findings

According to the NAACP, in 1995, California, Ohio, and Texas held nearly 40 percent of all the juveniles in custody in public facilities throughout the nation. Statistics on the number of children of color who are detained by the state are available for every state. For more information, contact the Washington Bureau of the NAACP at (202) 638-2269.

The NAACP reported in 1999 that minority children are incarcerated at disproportionate rates throughout the country. The organization discovered that:

- Although black children are only a third of country's child population, two-thirds of all incarcerated juveniles are considered ethnic minorities.
- In the black population, teenagers make up 15 percent, yet account for 26 percent of juvenile arrests in the country, 32 percent of delinquency referrals to juvenile court, 41 percent of juveniles detained in delinquency cases, 46 percent of juveniles in corrections institutions, and 52 percent of juveniles transferred to adult criminal court after judicial hearings.
- Minority youth are much more likely to end up in prisons with adult offenders.
- Between 1987 and 1991, out-of-home placements for children of color increased significantly for property, drug, and public-order offenses. This means that minority youth are more likely to be removed from their families than are their white counterparts.

NAACP Legislative Priorities

The Washington Bureau of the NAACP has listed a series of legislative issues that are important to its membership, and they are aggressively pursuing the issues. They are:

- **Passage of the Traffic Stops Statistics Study Act ("Driving While Black"):** Although this bill has passed the House, it never gets beyond the Senate.
- **Enhanced protection and prevention against hate crimes:** In the past, hate crimes tended to increase when the nation's economy was in a slump. However, in 1999, despite economic growth, hate crimes seem even more prevalent than predicted. Yet in the face of high-profile cases of hate crimes against minorities and gays in 1998—such as the beating death of Matthew Shepherd because he was gay—neither the House nor the Senate has passed the Hate Crimes Prevention Act. This legislation would make it easier for the federal government to assist in the investigation and prosecution of crimes motivated by the race, religion, national origin, gender, disability, or sexual preference of the victim.
- **Establishment of a police-accountability review board:** The NAACP would like to see the establishment of an effective review board on a national basis that would monitor police conduct and make sure that individual officers are accountable for their actions.

- **Ending racial disparity in death sentencing:** Capital punishment has always been biased against minorities, especially black Americans. In Philadelphia, the odds of receiving the death sentence are nearly four times higher if the defendant is African American, according to a recent study by the Death Penalty Information Center. The NAACP wants Congress to know that racial disparity in death sentences isn't new, nor is it confined to Philadelphia. This disparity exists throughout the country, and has since the beginning of slavery.

SENDING AN E-MAIL

To send an e-mail to your senator, go to www.senate.gov, click on "Senators," then click on "Contacting Senators" (by name or by state). This selection will also help you to identify the two senators from your state. And remember to contact both of your senators.

To send an e-mail to your House of Representatives, go to www.house.gov, and click on "Write Your Representative." This will help you identify who your congressperson is and how to contact him or her.

Another NAACP FYI

A growing movement to pass the Commission to Study Reparation Proposals for African Americans Act would authorize a government commission to explore the institution of slavery in America and its impact on current society and to make recommendations to

Congress for appropriate remedies. Passage of this bill would be an important first step in reparation for the cruelty, brutality, and inhumanity that slavery left behind in American society at the start of the new millennium.

BIBLIOGRAPHY

- "Anonymous Poem and U.S. Senator Charles E. Schumer's Senate Address" provided by the Press Office of U.S. Senator Charles E. Schumer (D-NY).
- "Disproportionate Minority Confinement," report by the 1999 Washington Bureau as presented at the 1999 NAACP 15th Annual Lawyers CLE Seminar held in New York, July 9–11, 1999.

CHAPTER 13

The American Civil Liberties Union Report

As a society, we do not have to choose between keeping people safe and treating them right, between enforcing the law and upholding civil rights. We can do both.
—President William Jefferson Clinton

On June 9, 1999, President Bill Clinton directed his cabinet and federal law-enforcement agencies to collect and report detailed data regarding traffic stops. The Justice Department will analyze the information and file a report that helps to identify positive ways to stop racial profiling. (The report will not be available until the summer of 2000.) The dilemma, unfortunately, is that only a fraction of our law enforcers actually work for the federal government. Most enforcement agencies fall under the jurisdiction of state and local governments, so the only real help President Clinton could offer would be to influence Congress to provide resources. For years, Representative John Conyers (D-MI) introduced his bill for the Traffic Stops Statistics Act that would require data collection, but his bill always gets killed in the Senate. The President had to step around Capitol Hill in order for the federal government to take action.

President Clinton remembered asking a group of black journalists how many had been the victims of racial profiling. Everyone raised a hand. Corporate attorneys, off-duty police officers, innocent grandparents, and many people reading this book, perhaps, have a story to tell. In the words of President Clinton, "Racial profiling is the opposite of good police work. It is wrong. It is destructive. And it must stop." In the news, the end to the war in Kosovo was within days, and in New York City, a police officer was convicted in the torture of Abner Louima, a Haitian immigrant who had become a national symbol of police brutality when he was assaulted in a Brooklyn police-station restroom. Three others were acquitted in that case.

Inside the Marriott Wardman Park Hotel in Washington, D.C., President Clinton ordered the Departments of Justice, Treasury, and the Interior to start collecting data on the race, ethnicity, and gender of individuals subject to traffic and pedestrian stops, inspections at entries into the U.S., and certain other searches by federal law-enforcement agencies—including the Immigration and Naturalization Service, Drug Enforcement Agency, Customs Service, and National Park Service—and after a year from June 9, 1999, to report on the findings of the new data-collection system and make recommendations based on those findings as to how to ensure greater fairness in federal law-enforcement procedures. In essence, President Clinton authorized the Justice Department to amend its National Crime Victimization Survey with questions about Americans' experiences with traffic stops, police use of force, and police misconduct. President Clinton had finally acknowledged the struggle, but not until after grassroots civil-rights organizations had already done the work.

> The 21st Century Policing Initiative contained in the President's crime bill has several monitory measures to help strengthen the integrity and ethics of police forces in communities across the country:
> - $20 million to expand police integrity and ethics training
> - $20 million for police scholarships to promote the best-educated police force possible
> - $2 million for improved minority recruitment to ensure that police departments reflect the diversity of the communities they represent
> - $10 million to help police departments purchase more video cameras to protect both the safety and the rights of individuals stopped and the safety of the officers making the stop
> - $5 million to establish citizen police academies to engage community residents in the fight against crime

When Robert Wilkins, the Washington, D.C., public defender, teamed up with the American Civil Liberties Union and initiated the lawsuit of *Robert L. Wilkins, et al.,* v. *Maryland State Police, et al.* in a District of Maryland courthouse, the national spotlight was placed on the practice of racial profiling. Together, Mr. Wilkins and the ACLU had made a few devastating discoveries concerning police conduct, and they presented their findings in a memorandum to the court. They had collected, organized, and analyzed data observed during the period between January 1995 and September 1996. David Harris, a law professor at the University of Toledo in Ohio, was the principal author of the report. (For the complete text of the report, visit the ACLU Web site at www.aclu.org/ profiling/report/index.html.) Mr. Harris found that the practice of systematic racial profiling became institutional- ized through a 1986 Drug Enforcement Agency program called Operation Pipeline, which trained over 27,000 police officers in forty-eight participating states. Each officer learned the use of pretext stops in order to find drugs in the car. And the worst part was that over the next ten years a series of Supreme Court decisions fueled the practice by allowing the police to use traffic stops as a pretext to "fish" for evi- dence of wrongdoing.

Sad, because traffic stops happen everywhere all the time. Millions of people of color have altered their driving habits and routes in efforts to avoid all-white suburbs. Young men have intentionally bought very plain-looking cars or become intensely conscious of the clothes they wear. And while mainstream America lived its life without a clue of what "driving while black" does to blacks on the road, the practice was allowed to grow into an institution. Middle class, upper class, poor, homeless, in school or out—it doesn't matter. Minorities all get profiled. Ask Christopher Darden, the black prosecutor in the O. J. Simpson trial. Mr. Darden spent fourteen years working with the police in prosecuting accused criminals, and even he publically admitted to having been racially profiled.

The ACLU report recounted more stories like the sto- ries you've read in this book, stories of motorists, pas- sengers, and pedestrians. However, there are certain legal requirements that must be met before a victim of profiling has his or her day in court. According to Reginald Shuford, the case must be more than "I was stopped; I'm black; therefore, I'm a victim of my race." As the point attorney in the ACLU's legal fight against racial profiling, he explains what else there must be.

"You have to have a colorable claim, a real chance to win your case, and evidence or some proof that what you alleged actually happened. Otherwise, the court would be inundated with frivolous cases of people who got pissed off, or someone with a grudge or a mean streak could file a claim. The courts have trouble dealing with the subject of race."

The fallacy that all black people are more likely to be involved with drugs fosters racial profiling across social lines. It makes it difficult to end the problem of profiling. It encourages the assumption by progressive and conservative people alike that there is a correlation between race and drugs. The reason blacks have higher statistics associating them with drug use results from certain elements that go into play once an officer stops a person. When white folks are stopped, they're given the benefit of the doubt; this benefit doesn't apply if a victim is black. One case that the ACLU is representing is of Alton Fitzgerald White, the former star of the Broadway musical *Ragtime*. He was walking out of his building on July 16, 1999, when he was stopped by police officers, patted down, taken to the 33rd Precinct police station and held for four hours and strip-searched. White, thirty-five, wasn't in a car, and he didn't have any drugs on him. And that is the problem with racial profiling as opposed to criminal profiling. The issue with racial profiling is that innocent people are the victims. Good folks who are not committing a crime are the ones stopped and questioned and harassed. The real victims are the people who are advancing up the economic ladder as doctors and lawyers and bankers and investors—people who are giving the black community a good name and image. On January 12, 2000, Mr. White filed a lawsuit against the NYPD as a result of his arrest.

San Diego Chargers football player Shawn Lee was pulled over in California in 1997. He and his girlfriend were handcuffed alongside Interstate 15 for over an hour and a half. The *Hartford Courant* and the *Boston Globe* published the Trumbull memo written by the chief of the all-white police force in Trumbull, Connecticut. Chief Theodore Amstrosini urged his force to take the offensive; if it meant developing a "sense of proclivity" toward the type of persons and vehicles, so be it. (Proclivity, by the way, means "an inclination or predisposition toward something; a strong inherent inclination toward something objectionable.") The Trumbull memo directed, "Not only is it our obligation to enforce the motor vehicle laws, but in doing so, we are provided with a profile of our community and those who travel within its boundaries." On Mother's Day in 1996, Alvin Penn, a black Bridgeport Democrat and deputy president in the state senate, was stopped.

Yawu Miller, a black reporter at the *Bay State Banner*, wanted to know how long it would take two black men driving together at night in a predominantly white community to get stopped by the police. He wrote that it happened "almost immediately."

Johnny Gammage was pulled over in Pennsylvania driving a Jaguar at two o'clock in the morning in 1996. Police ordered him out of the car. When Gammage reached for his cellular phone, the cops reacted and shot him. Gammage died at the scene. He was still handcuffed.

Story after story after story. A lot of people, a lot of stories. The ACLU concentrated on minority motorists. (The personal narratives published in this book show that racial profiling goes beyond the highways. It happens in everyday occurrences from shopping in the malls to walking through the park.) To date, the ACLU has filed various lawsuits challenging the police practice of racial profiling.

In the ACLU litigation of *Chavez* v. *Illinois State Police* (ISP), statistical data. helped the plaintiff show patterns of racially discriminatory traffic stops and searches. The ACLU reported that Illinois state troopers assigned to a drug-interdiction program called Operation Valkyrie had disproportionately singled out Hispanic motorists for discretionary offenses such as failure to signal a lane change or driving one to four miles over the speed limit. This is what they presented to the court:

- While Hispanics comprise less than 8 percent of the Illinois population and take fewer than 3 percent of the personal-vehicle trips in Illinois, they comprise 30 percent of the motorists stopped by the ISP drug-interdiction officers for traffic violations and 27 percent of the searches conducted by Valkyrie officers.
- While African Americans comprise less than 15 percent of the Illinois population and take approximately 10 percent of the personal-vehicle trips in Illinois, they comprise 23 percent of the searches conducted by Valkyrie officers. In that district, blacks are 24 percent of the local motorists, but are targets of searches 63 percent of the time.

- While troopers ask a higher percentage of Hispanic motorists than white motorists for a consent to search their car, they find contraband a lower percentage of the time.

In the early 1990s the U.S. Justice Department began an investigation into the 39th Police District of Philadelphia based on evidence that white officers were planting drugs on African Americans, assaulting them during arrests, and using illegal rules and procedures to prosecute and convict them. Although six officers were tried, convicted, and incarcerated for their criminal activities, the ACLU believed that the problem was far greater than just those six individuals. A series of mandates followed, including for the first time in this country a city's being forced to record information about traffic stops, including the reason for the stop, any police action taken, and the race of the driver. In July 1998 the ACLU issued its "Fourth Monitoring Report: Pedestrian and Car Stop Audit" based on data derived from a specific list of criteria.

For the week of March 7, 1997, of the 516 traffic stops reported, 262 identified racial or ethnic information about the motorists. Of these 262 stops, 85.9 percent were of minorities.

Asian	Black	Latino	White	Total
11	207	7	37	262
4.2%	79%	2.7%	14.1%	100%

The ACLU released data they had collected during the week of October 6, 1997, and found that of the 1,083 traffic stops, race was recorded in 524 instances, and of those

524 stops, 71.1 percent were of minorities. The numbers break down like this:

Asian	Black	Latino	White	Total
14	233	125	152	524
2.7%	44.5%	23.9%	29%	100%

American Civil Liberties Union
Driver-Profiling Complaint Form

By providing the information below, you are helping the American Civil Liberties Union collect much-needed data about the prevalence, patterns, and characteristics of racially discriminatory highway stops by state, county, and local police agencies. Please be assured that all personal information collected will be kept strictly confidential on request.

The ACLU cannot promise you that the information you provide will lead to any specific action on their part. But it is possible that you may receive a request from the ACLU or a state affiliate to use the information you have provided for one or more of the following purposes: (1) legislative testimony, (2) litigation, or (3) telling your story to the media.

If you were stopped in California, you may also wish to call the ACLU's California hotline at (877) DWB-STOP (392-7867). This number is for stops in California only. However, if you had a traffic stop in California, we encourage you to both call the number and provide the organization with the following information:

Information About You:
- First and last names
- Address: City, State, Zip
- Telephones: Home and office, fax, (e-mail, pager, mobile)
- Date of birth, sex, and occupation

The Traffic Stop

- Where the stop occurred (city and state)
- Date and time of day
- Make, model, and year of your vehicle

What Happened
- Give the exact location of the stop (street or highway) and your travel plan (points of origin and destination).
- Describe the events with as much detail as possible. Were you cited or ticketed? Were your license and registration checked? Were you asked to consent to a vehicular or personal search?
- If you refused a search, did the police take additional action? If you consented to the search, what happened? Was anything found (e.g., contraband such as weapons or drugs)?
- Do you believe you were stopped based on constitutionally protected characteristics such as your race or national origin? Did the officer specifically say or do anything to make you believe race played a factor? If so, indicate your race or national origin and explain the basis for this belief.
- Did you make a complaint to anyone about this

stop or search? If so, to whom did you make a complaint? What, if anything, was the response?
- If you were not ticketed or cited, was an explanation given for why you were stopped? If so, what explanation was given?
- What agency was the officer affiliated with (e.g., local police, state trooper, etc.)? If known, give the name(s) of police officer(s) who stopped you and/or name(s) of any witness(es):
- Were there any passengers in the vehicle in which you were riding or driving? If so, were they also questioned or searched? If so, explain in more detail, including their names and addresses, if appropriate.
- How long did the entire traffic stop take, and did the stop significantly disrupt your travel plans?

Uses of This Information

The ACLU may use your report to advocate legislative measures that will protect drivers from discriminatory traffic stops, or to identify jurisdictions where they may challenge race-based traffic stops in court.

Once again, submitting this information does not take the place of contacting your local ACLU office for assistance or representation.

Please mail or fax this information to the ACLU at:
ACLU National Office
125 Broad Street, 18th floor
New York, NY 10004
Attention: Driver-Profiling Complaint
Fax: (212) 549-2500

The ACLU provides a complaint form that you can download at their Freedom Network Web site: www.aclu.org/forms/trafficstops.html (copyright © 1998, the American Civil Liberties Union).

BIBLIOGRAPHY

- Webster's Ninth New Collegiate Dictionary, 1985.
- American Civil Liberties Union Press Material.

CHAPTER 14

The U.S. Department of Justice Addresses Police Misconduct

The U.S. Department of Justice's Civil Rights Division publishes a brochure entitled "Addressing Police Misconduct." It's important public information to have because it spells out the basic role that the DOJ plays in enforcing the laws of the United States that address police misconduct and explains how you as individual citizens can file a complaint with the DOJ if you believe that your rights have been violated. According to the DOJ, the vast majority of the law enforcement officers in the United States perform their jobs with respect to their communities and in compliance with the laws.

However, there are a few officers out there who are engaging in behavior that places them above the law . . .

Federal laws that address police misconduct include both criminal and civil statutes. These laws cover the action of state, county, and local officers, including those who work in prisons and jails. In addition, several of the laws apply to federal law-enforcement officers. The laws protect everyone within the borders of the United States, both citizens and noncitizens.

Each law the Department of Justice (DOJ) enforces is briefly discussed in this section. In DOJ investigations, whether criminal or civil, the person whose rights have reportedly been violated is referred to as a victim and is often an important witness. DOJ generally will inform the victim of the results of the investigation, but does not act as the victim's lawyer or attorney and cannot give legal advice as a private attorney could.

The various offices within DOJ that are responsible for enforcing the laws discussed in this section coordinate their investigation and enforcement efforts where appropriate. The example that the DOJ uses to illustrate this point is that a complaint received by one office will be referred to another office if necessary to address the allegations. Also, more than one office may investigate the same complaint if the allegation raise issues covered by more than one statue.

WHAT IS THE DIFFERENCE BETWEEN CRIMINAL AND CIVIL CASES?

Criminal and civil laws are different. Criminal cases usually are investigated and handled separately from civil cases, even if they concern the same incident. In a criminal case,

DOJ brings a case against the accused person; in a civil case, DOJ brings the case (either through litigation or an administrative investigation) against a governmental authority or law-enforcement agency. Also in a criminal case, the evidence must establish proof "beyond a reasonable doubt," while in civil cases the proof need only satisfy the lower legal standard of a "preponderance of the evidence." Finally, in criminal cases, DOJ seeks to punish a wrongdoer for past misconduct through imprisonment or other sanction. In civil cases, DOJ seeks to correct a law-enforcement agency's policies and practices that fostered the misconduct and, where appropriate, may require individual relief for the victim (or victims).

FEDERAL CRIMINAL ENFORCEMENT

It is a crime for one or more persons acting under the color of law to willfully deprive or conspire to deprive another person of any rights protected by the Constitution or laws of the United States. The "color of law" simply means that the person doing the act is using power given to him or her by a governmental agency (local, state, or federal). A law-enforcement officer acts "under color of law" even if he or she is exceeding his or her rightful power. The types of law-enforcement misconduct covered by Title VI include excessive force, sexual assault, intentional false arrest, or the intentional fabrication of evidence resulting in a loss of liberty to another. Enforcement of these provisions does not require that any racial, religious, or other discriminatory motive existed. (The officers indicted in the shooting of

the four young men en route to basketball tryouts were acting "under the color of law" when they racially profiled
the motorists and opened fire on the van.)

Violations of these laws are punishable by fine and/or
imprisonment. There is no private right of action under
these statutes; in other words, these are not the legal provisions under which you would file a lawsuit on your own.

FEDERAL CIVIL ENFORCEMENT: "POLICE MISCONDUCT"

Title VI makes it unlawful for state or local law-
enforcement officers to engage in a pattern or practice of
conduct that deprives a person of his or her rights as protected by the Constitution and laws of the United States.
The types of conduct covered by this law include, among
many other things, excessive force, discriminatory harassment, false arrest, coercive sexual conduct, and unlawful
stops, searches, or arrests. In order to be covered by this
law, the misconduct must constitute a "pattern or practice."
It cannot be simply an isolated incident. DOJ must be able
to show in court that a particular agency has an unlawful
policy or that the incidents constituted a pattern of unlawful conduct. However, unlike under the other civil laws discussed in this section, DOJ does not have to show that
discrimination has occurred in order to prove a pattern or
practice of misconduct.

DOJ may seek injunctive relief to end the misconduct and changes in the agency's policies and procedures
that resulted in, or allowed, the misconduct. The remedies

available under this law do not include individual monetary relief for the victims of the misconduct. There is no private right of action under this law; only DOJ may file suit for violations of the "Police Misconduct" Provision.

TITLE VI OF THE CIVIL RIGHTS ACT OF 1964 AND THE OJP PROGRAM STATUTE

Together, these laws prohibit discrimination on the basis of race, color, national origin, sex, and religion by state and local law-enforcement agencies that receive financial assistance from the Department of Justice. Currently, most communities are served by a law-enforcement agency that receives DOJ funds. These laws prohibit both individual instances and patterns and practices of discriminatory misconduct—such as treating a person differently because of race, color, national origin, sex, or religion. This misconduct covered by Title VI and the OJP (Office of Justice Programs) Program Statute includes harassment or use of racial slurs, unjustified arrests, discriminatory traffic stops, coercive sexual conduct, retaliation for filing a complaint with DOJ or participating in the investigation, use of excessive force, or refusal by the agency to respond to complaints alleging discriminatory treatment by its officers.

DOJ may seek changes in the policies and procedures of the agency to remedy violations of these laws and, if appropriate, also seek individual remedial relief for the victim (or victims). Individuals also have a private right of action under Title VI and under the OJP Program Statute; in other words, you may file a lawsuit yourself under these

laws. However, you must first exhaust your administrative
remedies by filing a complaint with DOJ if you wish to file
in federal court under the OJP Program Statute.

THE AMERICANS WITH DISABILITIES ACT AND SECTION 504 OF THE REHABILITATION ACT

Although the Americans with Disabilities Act (ADA)
doesn't directly relate to racial profiling, the subject of this
book, it does address the nature of discrimination. The
ADA and Section 504 prohibit similar forms of discrimination against specific individuals with disabilities on the basis
of the person's having a disability. These laws protect all
people with disabilities in the United States. A person is
considered to have a disability if he or she has a physical or
mental impairment that substantially limits one or more
major life activities, has a record of such an impairment, or
is regarded as having such an impairment.

The ADA prohibits discrimination on the basis of disability in all state and local governmental programs, services, and activities regardless of whether or not they
receive DOJ financial assistance; it also protects people who
are discriminated against because of their association with a
person with disability. Section 504 prohibits discrimination
by state and local law-enforcement agencies that receive
financial assistance from DOJ. It also prohibits discrimination in programs and activities conducted by federal agencies, including law-enforcement agencies.

These laws prohibit discriminatory treatment, including
misconduct, on the basis of disability in virtually all law-

enforcement services and activities. These activities include, among other things, interrogating witnesses, providing emergency services, enforcing laws, addressing citizen complaints, and arresting, booking, and holding suspects. These laws also prohibit retaliation for filing a complaint with DOJ or participating in the investigation.

If appropriate, DOJ may seek individual relief for the victim (or victims), in addition to changes in the policies and procedures of the law-enforcement agency. Individuals have a private right of action under both the ADA and Section 504; you may file a private lawsuit for violation of these statutes. Unlike procedures required for addressing police misconduct, there is no requirement that says you have to exhaust your administrative remedies before filing a complaint with DOJ first.

How to File a Complaint with DOJ

Criminal Enforcement

If you would like to file a complaint alleging a violation of the criminal laws discussed in this section, you may contact the Federal Bureau of Investigation (FBI), which is responsible for investigating allegations of criminal deprivations of civil rights. You may also contact the United States Attorney's Office (USAO) in your district. The FBI and USAO have public offices and publicly listed telephone numbers in most major cities.

In addition, you can send a written complaint to:
Criminal Section
Civil Rights Division

U.S. Department of Justice
P.O. Box 66018
Washington, D.C. 20035-6018

Civil Enforcement

If you elect to file a complaint alleging violations of the Police Misconduct Statute, Title VI, or the OJP Program Statute, you should send a written complaint to:

Coordination and Review Section
Civil Rights Division
U.S. Department of Justice
P.O. Box 66560
Washington, D.C. 20035-6560

You can also call the Coordination and Review Section's toll-free number for information and a complaint form at (888) 848-5306 (voice and TDD).

If you want to file a complaint alleging discrimination on the basis of disability, you can send a written complaint to:

Disability Rights Section
Civil Rights Division
U.S. Department of Justice
P.O. Box 66738
Washington, D.C. 20035-6738

You can also call the Disability Rights Section's toll-free ADA Information Line at (800) 514-0301 (voice) or (800) 514-0383 (TDD).

Q: How do I file a complaint about the conduct of a law-enforcement officer from a federal agency?

A: If you believe that you are a victim of racial profiling or some other criminal misconduct by a law-enforcement officer from a federal agency (such as the Immigration and Naturalization Service [INS]; the FBI; the Customs Service; Alcohol, Tobacco and Firearms; or the Border Patrol), you should follow the procedures and send a complaint to the Coordination and Review Section at the address listed above. That office will assign your complaint to the appropriate division and office. (States have similar procedures and protocols.)

Q: What information should I include in a complaint to DOJ?

A: Your complaint, whether alleging violations of criminal or civil laws listed in this section, should include the following information:

- Your name, address, and telephone number(s)
- The name(s) of the law-enforcement agency (or agencies) involved
- A description of the conduct you believe violated the laws discussed in this section, in as much detail as possible without going overboard. You should include: the dates and times of the incident(s); any injuries sustained; the name(s) or other identifying information of the officer(s) involved, if possible, and any other examples of similar misconduct.
- The name(s) and telephone number(s) of the witness(es)
- If you believe that the misconduct was based on your race, color, national origin, sex, religion, or disability, identify the basis and explain what leads

you to believe that you were treated in a discriminatory manner (differently from persons of another race, sex, etc.).

BIBLIOGRAPHY

• Source: The U.S. Department of Justice.

CHAPTER 15

Know Your Bill
of Rights

Remember that Negroes, Latinos, Native Americans, Chinese, women—white or black—and children (to name only a few) were never protected by the original 1776 interpretation of the United States Constitution and the Bill of Rights. It took black Americans 173 years—and a lot of innocent blood shed—before Congress used its power to enforce appropriate legislation that truly recognized blacks and other minorities as covered by the Constitution.

Over the course of American history, minorities have been granted specific protection by the Constitution, but only because specific people have brought specific cases before the American judiciary system. In court, one person can initiate a case that changes the whole American legal system. With respect to black history, long before Dr. Martin Luther King, Jr., and the passage of the civil-rights legislation in the 1960s, Thurgood Marshall and the NAACP Legal Defense Fund were breaking down walls through the courts very much the same way that Reginald Shuford and the ACLU are doing today. Minorities have had long histories marching through the streets rallying for justice. The Reverend Al Sharpton is always involved in a protest march or demonstration in some New York City neighborhood. Marching through the streets demanding justice is great for a "call to arms"—so to speak—among the masses, but if you want to change the American legal system, take your case to court. These days it's hard for a march to truly affect the American legal system.

Every American citizen should memorize the Bill of Rights and related amendments. Citizens have rights. And when they are violated, the victim has a right to redress. We maintain that if private resolution and settlement don't resolve any dispute of racism or racial profiling, then legal action is the only available option. The Constitution allows this. Filing a civil lawsuit within the United States court system against a person, an employer, or an institution you feel violated your rights, or registering a grievance or complaint with the Department of Justice can sometimes be more effective in changing public policy than a thousand marches of a million people at the footsteps of Capitol Hill.

Now that all Americans are protected under today's legal interpretation of the Constitution, its introduction finally speaks to every citizen: "We the People of the United States, in Order to form a more perfect Union, establish Justice, insure domestic Tranquillity, provide for the common defense, promote the general Welfare, and secure the Blessings of Liberty to ourselves and our Posterity, do ordain and establish this Constitution for the United States of America."

Unfortunately as the year 2000 gets started, racial issues that divided the country in 1863 and in 1963 still divide us. Anyone want to bet on the year 2063?

Bill of Rights

(Amendments One through Ten were ratified December 15, 1791.)

First Amendment

Congress shall make no law respecting an establishment of religion, or prohibiting the free exercise thereof; or abridging the freedom of speech, or of the press; or the right of the people to peaceably assemble, and to petition the Government for a redress of grievances.

Second Amendment

A well regulated Militia being necessary to the security of a free State, the right of the people to keep and bear Arms shall not be infringed.

Third Amendment

No Soldier shall, in time of peace, be quartered in any house, without the consent of the Owner, nor in time of war, but in a manner to be prescribed by law.

Fourth Amendment

The right of the people to be secure in their persons, houses, papers, and effects, against unreasonable searches and seizures, shall not be violated, and no Warrants shall issue, but upon probable cause, supported by Oath or affirmation, and particularly describing the place to be searched, and the persons or things to be seized.

Fifth Amendment

No person shall be held to answer for a capital, or otherwise infamous crime, unless on a presentment or indictment of a Grand Jury, except in cases arising in the land or naval forces, or in the Militia, when in actual service in time of War or public danger; nor shall any person be subject for the same offense to be twice put in jeopardy of life or limb; nor shall be compelled in any criminal case to be a witness against himself, nor be deprived of life, liberty, or property, without due process of law; nor shall private property be taken for public use, without just compensation.

Sixth Amendment

In all criminal prosecutions, the accused shall enjoy the right to a speedy and public trial, by an impartial jury of the State and district wherein the crime shall have been committed, which district shall have been previously ascertained by law, and to be informed of the nature and cause of the accusation; to be confronted with the witnesses against him; to have compulsory process for obtaining witnesses in his favor, and to have the Assistance of Counsel for his defense.

Seventh Amendment

In suits at common law, where the value in controversy shall exceed twenty dollars, the right of trial by jury shall be preserved, and no fact tried by a jury, shall be otherwise reexamined in any Court of the United States, than according to the rules of the common law.

Eighth Amendment
Excessive bail shall not be required, nor excessive fines imposed, nor cruel and unusual punishments inflicted.

Ninth Amendment
The enumeration in the Constitution, of certain rights, shall not be construed to deny or disparage others retained by the people.

Tenth Amendment
The powers not delegated by the United States by the Constitution, nor prohibited by it to the States, are reserved to the States respectively, or to the people.

Additional Relevant Amendments to the Constitution

Thirteenth Amendment, Section One
(Ratified December 6, 1865)
Neither slavery nor involuntary servitude, except as a punishment for crime whereof the party shall have been duly convicted, shall exist within the United States, or any place subject to their jurisdiction.

Fourteenth Amendment, Sections One and Two
(Ratified July 9, 1868)
Section One: All persons born or naturalized in the United States, and subject to the jurisdiction thereof, are citizens of the United States and of the State wherein they reside. No State shall make or enforce any law which shall abridge the privileges or immunities of citizens of the United States; nor shall any State deprive any person of life, liberty, or property, without due process of law; nor deny to any person within its jurisdiction the equal protection of the laws.

Section Two: Representatives shall be apportioned among the several States according to their respective numbers, counting the whole number of persons in each State, excluding Indians not taxed. But when the right to vote at any election for the choice of electors for President and Vice-President of the United States, Representatives in Congress, the Executive and Judicial officers of a State, or the members of the Legislature thereof, is denied to any of the male inhabitants of such State, being twenty-one years of age, and citizens of the United States, or in any way abridged, except for participation in rebellion, or other crime, the basis of representation therein shall be reduced in the proportion which the number of such male citizens shall bear to the whole number of male citizens twenty-one years of age in such State.

Fifteenth Amendment, Sections One and Two
(Ratified February 3, 1870)
Section One: The right of citizens of the United States to vote shall not be denied or abridged by the United States or by any State on account of race, color, or previous condition of servitude.

Section Two: The Congress shall have power to enforce this article by appropriate legislation.

Nineteenth Amendment, Sections One and Two
(Ratified August 18, 1920)
Section One: The right of citizens of the United States to vote shall not be denied or abridged by the United States or by any State on account of sex.

Section Two: Congress shall have power to enforce this article by appropriate legislation.

Twenty-Sixth Amendment, Sections One and Two
(Ratified July 1, 1971)
Section One: The right of citizens of the United States, who are eighteen years of age or older, to vote shall not be denied or abridged by the United States or by any State on account of age.

Section Two: The Congress shall have power to enforce this article by appropriate legislation.

In the Public Eye

From the moment you step out of your house, you should consider yourself in public. Someone is seeing you. And depending on who's watching, that someone just might be judging you. You can be buying groceries in your neighborhood supermarket, or having dinner with family in a restaurant, or just walking down the street going home, and you can be the victim of "something while black." When you are, it's crucial that you recognize it. In public places like schools, parks, libraries, and restaurants, it is against federal law to discriminate on the basis of race, color, religion, national origin, or disability in any public facility.

Similarly, your employer cannot discriminate against you on these same bases in:
- hiring, firing, promotion, or discipline
- the conditions and terms of your employment when compared to other employees
- harassing you, or allowing other employees to harass you

- creating or allowing you to work in a hostile or offensive work environment (for example, you have a right to work where racist jokes are not told)

Other Matters of Race

A few more discriminatory practices that are prohibited on the state and local level are:

- Redlining—the refusal of a bank to provide a mortgage for anyone within a certain geographical area.
- Blockbusting—the exploitation of racial prejudice to lower the selling prices of houses within an area.
- Steering—showing homes based on the race, color, religion, or national origin of the buyer.
- Restrictive covenants—clauses in a contract, for example, that prohibit the sale of property to members of a certain racial, religious, or ethnic group.

In related matters of housing, federal law prohibits discrimination.

- when buying or renting housing
- in advertising for the rental or purchase of a home
- in mortgage lending and home financing
- in brokerage services

FILE YOUR CLAIM

The word "file" should be forever etched in your mind. It's a tool you should use when you feel your rights have been violated.

- File a charge with the U.S. Department of Justice.
- File a charge with your state's human-rights commission.
- File a legal suit.

BIBLIOGRAPHY

- *We Can All Get Along: Fifty Steps You Can Take to Help End Racism,* by Clyde W. Ford (Dell, 1994).

CHAPTER 16

Proactive Steps

he most important step has already been made: The problem of racial profiling has received national attention.

Communication is everything! Without it, the struggle would be in vain.

In 1991, my nineteen-year-old nephew Damani Higgins and his twenty-one-year-old friend were walking along Frederick Douglass Boulevard at 136th Street in Harlem in the wee hours of the morning, when it happened. They were heading home from an evening with friends and were pretty tired. For Damani, the walk was one he had made a thousand times before, from the C train to the apartment we shared. It was Damani's friend's first visit to Damani's apartment. The young men, both of whom had dreadlocks, knapsacks, baggy clothes, and a Generation X attitude, had just crossed the street, when suddenly two strangers appeared, seemingly out of nowhere.

"Yo, yo, wait right here," one of the men said to Damani, flashing a gun he held next to his stomach.

Damani didn't need to see the gun to recognize he was being robbed.

The other stranger pointed his gun at Damani's friend. "Keep walking, kid!"

He moved on, turning around every few paces to make sure he wasn't going to be shot in the back. Meanwhile, Damani remained calm.

"My man," Damani said disarmingly. He held his hands in the air, waving the young men off. "Whatever you want, it's yours." Damani took off his brand-new headphones with the thick rubber padding and handed them over. "Here, the Walkman's inside my backpack."

"Give it up, slim."

Damani handed over his backpack.

The whole armed robbery didn't take longer than two minutes, it seemed. When the strangers, who were young (no more than a couple of years older than Damani), tall, and slim, got what they wanted, they disappeared inside a waiting Maxima with New York license plates. Apparently the driver had been monitoring the whole robbery from a close distance. As the car drove off, Damani could see, aside from the two men who actually robbed them, the driver and another man in the backseat.

As the friends watched the car disappear down the avenue, they caught their breath and immediately flagged down a passing police cruiser.

"We just got robbed," the young men told the officers, who never bothered to get out of their car.

"Aaww," one of the white officers answered sarcastically, "Milli Vanilli got robbed."

It wasn't the response the young men expected, but they swallowed their pride and didn't make an issue of it. They filed a report and rode around the neighborhood in the backseat of the police car, looking for the dark Maxima.

This little anecdote isn't to say young black men rob other young black men. We know that. But communication is everything! It's about how these white officers responded to Damani's experience.

When Damani and his friend walked through the apartment door early that morning, furious at being robbed, his friend said that walking away from the robbery feeling that they might be shot in the back wasn't the worst part of the experience. It was the officers calling them Milli Vanilli. The officers' response sparked a dialogue about the ills of white police officers patrolling black neighborhoods. Without communication, the struggle is in vain. As always, communication is the first and most important step in any relationship.

On the morning of May 12, 1999, Hilary O. Shelton testified before the House Judiciary Committee on Police Misconduct with Chairman Henry Hyde and ranking member John Conyers. On behalf of the NAACP, he told the committee that police misconduct has been a long-standing problem in this nation. And despite high-profile cases of police abuse making their way into the national attention, particularly in the past couple of years, the problem isn't anything new. As an organization, the NAACP has demonstrated in front of the U.S. Department of Justice, on the steps of Capitol Hill, and even at the doors of the Supreme Court, and at the heart of each demonstration is this simple message:

"We are just growing increasingly weary of being treated as criminals or suspected criminals simply because we are walking down the street, driving a car, or sitting on our front porch. The NAACP feels very strongly that we must take concrete and decisive action now to ensure that our sons and daughters do not become victims of police brutality or the mistrust and hatred that it breeds."

Shelton testified that the NAACP discovered that a wall of mistrust existed between minority groups and the police, and that the relationship was continuously in decline. Sarcastic remarks by white officers to black victims of armed robbery don't help. When the organization examined the origins of the breakdown of respect and cooperation, they also found that racism, "the combination of racial prejudice plus power and intolerance for different cultures," was a major ingredient to police misconduct and abusive use of force. Black Americans have always thought that police officers treat every minority as either criminals or potential criminals, and it's interactions like that between Damani, his friend, and the police officers that perpetrate the perception of mistrust and ill will. A solution to this particular problem is to require that inner-city police officers live in inner-city neighborhoods. Otherwise, Hilary Shelton explained, the continued practice of inner-city police officers living in white suburban communities makes them seem like a U.S. military force occupying a foreign country.

"The issue of racial profiling is finally beginning to gain much deserved media attention as of late," Shelton testified.

"It is, however, a problem that has been with our nation for as far back as our collective African American recollections can take us. No matter what the age group, from seventeen to ninety-seven, and no matter what region of the country you survey, nearly everyone has a story to tell of unfair treatment by the police [that is] based on racial identification. The conclusion should not be surprising to non-minority members of this Congress: Racial profiling is blatantly unjust, and because it has been a fact of life in our communities for so long, it has fostered a mistrust of the police, and consequently, the American judicial system as a whole."

So what's the solution?

There isn't a simple solution. The NAACP, ACLU, and the New Jersey state attorney general's office offer a variety of answers that must be considered. If you really want to know a possible solution for your particular neighborhood or community, ask your neighbor, your nearby family members, your community leaders and activists, or your elected officials. As a complete, national comprehensive package, there aren't enough pages in any book to offer you the total answer. So among the hundreds of thousands of people who have been victims of racial profiling and who also have a practical contribution to its solution, this chapter offers a few proactive steps that you can take to help end profiling. Hilary Shelton testified to the obvious: "We need comprehensive packages at the federal, state, and local levels that address the issues. We also need elected officials, police-union executives, and people in positions of authority to commit themselves to ridding our nation of this scourge."

The President and the U.S. Attorney General have

already mandated that the Department of Justice begin proactive steps in reviewing police-brutality cases. The NAACP, under a strong push from its president and CEO, Kweisi Mfume, convinced the federal government to commit resources to this cause. The White House established a uniform set of criteria for police stop-and-frisk procedures, profiling of suspects, and strip searches of suspects.

> Representatives from the National Urban League, National Leadership Forum, Anti-Defamation League, Human Rights Coalition, Rainbow Coalition, Leadership Conference on Civil Rights, and the National Asian-Pacific American Consortium also participated with the NAACP in its meetings with U.S. Attorney General Janet Reno.

The ACLU, a nationwide, nonpartisan organization of 275,000 members dedicated to preserving and defending the principles set forth in the Bill of Rights, also has a four-part battle plan against the "scourge of racial profiling." Their report, "Driving While Black: Racial Profiling on Our Nation's Highway" (May 1999), claims that most of the complaints they get regarding "driving while black" cases involve the use of traffic stops for non-traffic purposes, usually drug interdiction. And since the Supreme Court won't rule the practice of pretextual stops unconstitutional, the ACLU calls on the individual law-enforcement professional to use his or her best professional judgment in scrutinizing the wisdom of the pretext-stop tactic."

For this reason, the ACLU wants to see the passage of the Traffic Stops Statistics Study Act. As already mentioned, it would require the collection of several categories of data on individual traffic stops, including the race of the driver and whether or not a search was conducted. Minority citizens must light a fire under the seats of Democratic and Republican congressional leaders to pass key legislation. If they just followed through and funded the provision of the Crime Control Act of 1994, that itself would allow for the accurate, comprehensive collection of data on the use of excessive force by the police, including data on the number of people killed or injured by police shootings and other types of force. Although provisions have been mandated, it has yet to be funded. The last initiative is to get states to work together, preferably through the Conference of Governors, to develop a uniform set of procedures and a process for the establishment of countrywide police civilian-review boards that have both subpoena and investigatory powers. This protects the minority community from the police.

Another contribution to the solution of racial profiling is for each individual state to follow the lead of North Carolina and Connecticut and pass its own legislation on traffic stops. The ACLU would also like to see the fifty largest American cities voluntarily collecting traffic-stop data as well. San Diego's chief of police announced in February 1999 that his department would begin to collect data on traffic stops without any federal or state requirement to do so. In March, the San Jose Police Department announced similar record-keeping, and in April, the Portland police chief collected signatures from twenty-three Oregon police agencies that made a commitment to collect traffic-stop data.

Ten Principles to an Effective
Civilian-Review Board

The NAACP strongly believes that a police-accountability review board would help identify the few law-enforcement officers who are actively engaged in the practice of racial profiling. Along with the ACLU and various other grassroots and civil-rights organizations, the NAACP released a statement that includes what they believe are the ten principles for an effective civilian-review board. Those principles are:

- **Independence.** The power to conduct hearings, subpoena witnesses and report findings and recommendations to the public.
- **Investigatory power.** The authority to independently investigate incidents and issue findings on complaints.
- **Mandatory police cooperation.** Complete access to police witnesses and documents through legal mandate or subpoena power.
- **Adequate funding.** Should not be lower-budget priority than police internal-affairs systems.
- **Hearings.** Essential for solving credibility questions and enhancing public confidence in the process.
- **Reflection of community diversity.** The board and staff should be broadly representative of the community they serve.
- **Policy recommendations.** Civilian oversight can spot problem policies and provide a forum for developing reforms.

- **Statistical analysis.** Public statistical reports can detail trends in allegations, and early-warning systems can identify officers who are subjects of unusually numerous complaints.
- **Separate offices.** Should be housed away from police headquarters to maintain independence and credibility with the public.
- **Disciplinary role.** Board findings should be considered in determining appropriate disciplinary action.

According to the ACLU, in 1997, California Highway Patrol canine units stopped nearly 34,000 vehicles. Only 2 percent of them were carrying drugs. Law-enforcement decisions based on hunches rather than evidence are going to suffer from racial stereotyping, whether conscious or unconscious. The ACLU has a nationwide driving while black hotline for victims at (877) 6-PROFILE.

Sen. Charles Schumer (D-NY) offered a possible solution for New York City police officers that could be instituted across the country. It's a simple principle: Put into place a system that quickly relieves bad cops of police duty. Justin Volpe was one of the police officers accused in the torture case of Haitian immigrant Abner Louima. He had "multiple complaints against him" long before he became a national symbol of police brutality. It was also well known that officer Francis Livoti was a ticking time bomb years before he strangled Anthony Baez in 1994. In the senator's opinion, the NYPD knew about him, yet did nothing to relieve him of duty. The attitude of silence—protecting your own by sweeping problems under the rug—has got to end, not only for the sake of future victims but for the department itself. It is in the interest of any victim of racial profiling to end the policy of silence.

Senator Schumer said within the walls of the nation's Capitol that various mayors from various cities, along with police chiefs, police-union leaders, community leaders, and church leaders have to urge police officers to come forward when they spot a bad seed on the force. He wants society to consider it an honorable action, nothing shameful. There has to be an opportunity for people to report trouble-makers; when they do, there become fewer victims. Because most crimes in individual neighborhoods are committed by a few people, he said this whistle-blowers' protection policy would reduce the number of stop-and-frisk procedures so widely practiced in cities like New York.

"When there is an open line of communication, and a reporting of abusive or disrespectful officers, the quality of minority rights increases," he said in his first formal address to the Senate.

Nothing good comes of a young black man once he enters the criminal-justice system. In 1999, Pennsylvania State University discovered that the perceptions that judges have toward young black men seriously affect their sentencing. In fact, young African American males receive more severe jail sentences than do women and older offenders— white and black—because judges perceive them as more dangerous and less reformable, according to researchers Dr. Darrell J. Steffensmeier and Dr. John H. Kramer, professors of sociology at Penn State. Together, they, with Dr. Jeffrey Ulmer, assistant professor of sociology at Purdue University, are co-authors of the paper "The Interaction of Race,

Gender and Age in Criminal Sentencing: The Punishment Cost of Being Young, Black and Male," which recently appeared in the journal *Criminology*. Dr. Darrell J. Steffensmeier said that black men in their twenties and thirties are less likely to be viewed as societal victims than are other age and gender groups. And while the primary determinants of a judge's sentencing decisions are the seriousness of the crime and the defendant's prior record, the three factors of race, age, and gender clearly play a significant role.

These researchers discovered that the criminal records of young black males were often defined as qualitatively more serious and more indicative of future crime risk compared to those of other types of defendants, including older black offenders. And women and older offenders were seen as posing less danger to community safety than were younger black males, so they stayed out of jail more. But they also found, according to a spokesman for the three researchers, that courts in general tended to view women and older offenders as more expensive to the correctional system in terms of health care and child welfare. Women and older offenders were seen as having more ties to the community, more likely to be supporting a family and more likely to have a steady job, currently and in the future. Young black males, however, were seen as lacking such social bonds, which insulate individuals from future criminal involvement. Indicators of stability and conventionality such as employment or care of others were more likely to favor female defendants and less likely to favor young black male defendants. All of this is a form of "driving while black" as perpetrated by court judges and trial lawyers.

NEW YORK CITY BRONX
DISTRICT ATTORNEY

Bronx district attorney Robert Johnson was the first black DA elected in the state of New York. In February 1999, when four police officers shot Amadou Diallo nineteen times out of forty-one shots, it was Robert Johnson's responsibility to convene a grand jury. The controversy surrounding that shooting was politically charged. As an elected official who works for the state of New York, the same state that employed the NYPD, the mayor and the governor, Mr. Johnson had to walk a thin tightrope. It was almost a conflict of interest. Anyone who knows the setup of the district attorney's office knows that he is dependent on police officers to help him win cases, and if he turns too quickly on any one officer—"quick to convict"—he might lose support of the police department, which means he would lose the many cases that are dependent on police officers to testify on his office's behalf. That wouldn't help him in his reelection bid.

Robert Johnson was elected to a four-year term on November 8, 1988, another in 1992, and one more in 1996. In 1986 he was appointed to a judgeship in the New York City criminal-courts system and promoted to acting justice on the state supreme court. A native New Yorker, Robert Johnson relates to today's high-school students, speaking at local high schools about youth and the criminal-justice system. As the Bronx DA, Johnson runs a law office of 800 staff members with over 400 attorneys (over 120 are lawyers of color, and half of them are women [as of fall

1999]). In 1998 his office handled more than eighty thousand cases. Mr. Johnson says he's in the best possible position to protect his community—by prosecuting the guilty. Before he lets another young black man stand before a judge, he goes over the facts of the case and makes a decision as to whether there is enough evidence to warrant going to court.

"Doing justice means not only prosecuting the guilty, but it also means weeding things out and making sure we're not persecuting the innocent," says Johnson in the aftermath of the Amadou Diallo shooting.

The Officers Who Opened Fire on Amadou Diallo

On Friday, February 5, 1999, the *New York Post* published a short fact list of the four members of New York City's elite Street Crime's Unit involved in the shooting. They are:

- Officer Kenneth Boss, twenty-seven, seven years on the force, with twenty-three Excellent Police Duty awards. On October 31, 1997, Boss shot a man three times, killing him. While on duty, he confronted the suspect, who was pointing a shotgun at him in East New York. He had three Citizen Complaints Review Board (CCRB) complaints against him.

- Officer Richard Murphy, twenty-six, five years on the force, with two Excellent Police Duty awards. With no complaints against him during his tenure, he fired only four times in the Diallo shooting.

- Officer Sean Carroll, thirty-five, six years on the

force. With three complaints filed against him with the CCRB, he emptied his clip during the Diallo shooting (sixteen rounds).

- Officer Edward McMellon, twenty-six, five years on the force, with three Excellent Police Duty awards and no complaints. He also fired sixteen rounds during the Diallo shooting. In June 1998 he shot an armed suspect once in the torso in East New York. It was ruled justified.

REMEDIAL STEPS

The New Jersey state attorney general's "Interim Report" offers remedial steps toward ending racial profiling. Some of the policies and procedures that office described in the report are new, while others are reaffirmations or clarifications of existing State Police policies and practices. These ideas can easily apply to all fifty states.

- Along New Jersey highways, the Standard Operating Procedures manual governing motor-vehicle stops requires that state troopers have a reasonable, articulable suspicion that evidence of a crime would be found before asking for permission to conduct a search. It also requires that all consents to search be reduced to writing.
- State troopers are required to advise the dispatcher at central command as to the racial characteristics of motorists who are stopped. Recording this information also in the troopers' patrol logs prohibits the practice of "spotlighting" or "ghosting" vehicles of white motorists. Spotlighting is the practice of patrol officers logging the

license plate numbers of passing white motorists on the ticket given to blacks. (The troopers indicted in the shooting of black motorists on their way to basketball tryouts were charged with this crime.)

- Requiring state troopers to be equipped with video cameras to record reliable and trustworthy accounts of police encounters. Some patrol cars are currently equipped with video cameras.

The constitutional requirement of reasonableness—the foundation of all Fourth Amendment jurisprudence—is satisfied, literally, when a government actor can articulate legitimate and sufficient reasons to justify an invasion of privacy or intrusion upon a private citizen's recognized liberty interest. For the most part, our recommendations would not actually restrict the exercise of police discretion, but rather would only require an officer to be prepared to explain the reasons for his or her discretionary decisions. This is hardly an unreasonable or insuperable impediment to effective law enforcement.

—Attorney General Peter Verniero's
"Interim Report," 1999

SPECIFIC ACTIONS AS PROPOSED BY ATTORNEY GENERAL VERNIERO AND FIRST ASSISTANT ATTORNEY GENERAL ZOUBEK

- **Updated statewide drug-enforcement strategy.** The attorney general's office recommends issuing an updated statewide drug-enforcement strategy to define the enforcement priorities and contributions of all law-enforcement agencies as part of a comprehensive response to New Jersey's drug problem.

- **Quarterly publication of State Police statistics.** The Department of Law and Public Safety should prepare and make public on a quarterly basis aggregate statistics compiled pursuant to the databases created in accordance with the recommendations of the attorney general's "Interim Report."
- **Revise the standard operating procedures for traffic stops.** There should be a uniformed updated procedural manual that supersedes all Standard Operating Procedures (SOP) regarding traffic stops. In preparing the revised SOP, the attorney general's office suggests that the following steps be considered: 1) the trooper should inform the dispatcher of the exact reason for the motorist stop before the trooper exits the patrol car; 2) creating a system to monitor the duration of all stops; 3) requiring that all video cameras be activated before the trooper exits the patrol car and not turned off until the detained car has been released; 4) requiring the trooper to introduce him- or herself by name and inform the driver as to the reason for the stop; 5) when the stop has concluded, the trooper will inform the dispatcher as to the outcome, which must be done before the trooper leaves the scene; 6) every traffic stop must be logged into a Traffic Stop Report form, which records all officer action for immediate supervisory review.
- **Develop practical stop criteria.** This would require a comprehensive set of criteria to be used by state troopers

in exercising the officer's discretion in selecting vehicles to be stopped.

- **Establish procedures governing consent searches.** This requires a police chief to replace, update, and supersede all existing SOP regarding consent searches. The revised procedure will reaffirm the existing policy that troopers must request permission to conduct a search only when facts are present that constitute a reasonable, articulable suspicion that the search will uncover evidence of a crime. This would require: 1) All state troopers must use a Search Incident Form (SIF) in an effort to document and record a motor-vehicle search. 2) The SIF must provide that all consent searches require written authorization before any search is initiated. 3) Written authorization on the SIF must be obtained before a search starts. 4) The SIF must be completed whether or not permission to search was granted. 5) No searches shall be conducted on the basis of verbal or "implied" consent. 6) State troopers must advise any person being asked to give permission to search that he or she is free to leave when, in fact, such is the case. 7) The SIF should specifically inform the person being asked to give permission to search that he or she has the right to be present during the consent search. 8) The immediate supervisor of the trooper initiating a search is responsible to review the circumstances and outcome of the incident within twenty-four hours. 9) When a police cruiser is equipped with a video camera, the entire search must be recorded.

- **Require a state trooper to inform dispatcher of his or her intention to conduct a probable-cause search.** Because probable-cause searches are, by definition, bona fide criminal investigations based on an objective assessment that a search would reveal contraband or evidence of a crime, a patrol supervisor should ordinarily be dispatched to the scene and should be present prior to the execution of the search when feasible.

> Although the racial profiling issue has gained state and national attention recently, the underlying conditions that foster disparate treatment of minorities have existed for decades in New Jersey and throughout the nation, and will not be changed overnight.
> —Attorney General Verniero's "Interim Report"

BIBLIOGRAPHY

- "The Officers Who Opened Fire," compiled by Rocco Parascandola, Murray Weiss, and Larry Celona (*New York Post*, February 5, 1999).

CHAPTER 17

The Problem with Hailing a Taxi

An evening with friends and family that costs over five hundred dollars, and feels every bit of a thousand dollars, can be deflated into pennies when you go out at night and can't hail a cab.
—Kenneth Meeks

ormer New York City Mayor David Dinkins, State Senator David Paterson, singer Lenny Kravitz, comedian Chris Rock, film director Spike Lee, and thousands of other famous and not-so-famous black men and women who may or may not have officially reported the experience all have something in common, and it can happen on any given night or any given day, in any given year. If you're a black man or woman who happens to be in Chicago, New York City, Philadelphia, Los Angeles, and a few other cities in between, go outside tonight and try this experiment: Hail a taxi. You will eventually get one, but not before one or two pass you by.

In early October 1999, superstar actor Danny Glover, his

daughter Mandisa (a senior at New York University at the time), and her friend had an entire evening start and end with disastrous cab stories. His celebrity status brought the age-old problem of blacks' being ignored by cabbies back into the limelight. The *Daily News,* the *New York Post,* and the *New York Times* picked up on Glover's story only when he decided to go public with a formal complaint a month later. New York City reacted. The Taxi and Limousine Commission (TLC), along with the New York Police Department, set up sting operations to catch and fine taxi drivers who pass minorities on the streets. A few other organizations reacted in their own ways, too. The Reverend Al Sharpton and the National Action Network filed a class-action lawsuit against the TLC, and minority officers within the NYPD and members of 100 Blacks in Law Enforcement campaigned to get more officers onto the street issuing summonses to taxi drivers who illegally pass black and Hispanic customers.

The stories are straightforward and predictable. And the victims are people of color from every walk of life. In the case of Danny Glover and his daughter, they were discriminated against six times in one evening. Leaving his daughter's apartment building at 116th Street and Seventh Avenue in Harlem, Glover said at a news conference held in the lobby of the TLC offices, five Yellow Cabs refused to pick them up, and on their way home a sixth taxi driver refused to allow Glover to ride up front in the passenger seat. Cabdrivers are required to allow passengers up front if a passenger has a physical need. At six feet four, Glover had to sit up front because of a bad hip.

More than 320 taxi drivers were convicted in 1998 of service refusals, carrying penalties ranging from $320 in fines to revocation of a driver's license. TLC Commissioner Diane McGrath-McKechnie said the number would be higher if New Yorkers who initiate civil-rights complaints against taxi drivers followed up by attending the hearing with the driver or having the matter adjudicated. The number of convictions is low because the TLC is forced to drop the charges when complainants don't appear. The TLC received 2,317 service-refusal complaints between July 1998 and June 1999, yet 71 percent of the complainants failed to appear to the follow-up hearings, whereupon the case gets automatically dismissed.

Ellis Cose, a successful black journalist who wrote the book *The Rage of a Privileged Class* (HarperCollins, 1994), made an interesting point in the *New York Times* about hailing a cab. He said people generally assume all whites are middle class until they prove themselves different, while blacks and Latinos are generally assumed *not* to be middle class until they prove it. "If a black guy in a suit goes to the downtown side of Broadway, his chances of hailing a cab, say, go from maybe 15 percent to 40 percent, compared to the guy not dressed professionally and going uptown."

And although the press tend to focus on black men who can't hail a cab, it's equally important to not lose sight of reality: Black women have just as much a problem catching cabs as men. Danny Glover's daughter Mandisa was reportedly having trouble hailing a taxi that night in October, too. Women get ignored in department stores, get seated in the back of elegant restaurants, and are bypassed by cabbies just as black men are. One *New York Times* reporter agreed with the basic premise of this book: "All my African American and brown-skinned Latino acquaintances have stories," the reporter wrote. "They come home from work in a suit and tie and a neighbor asks if they are delivering groceries. The doorman who is so friendly to the other tenants harasses or ignores them and their black and Hispanic friends. The service is a tad off in the best restaurants. They are mistaken for the help in exclusive stores." So don't believe that sisters in a skirt can get a taxi any better than black men can. Cabdrivers don't discriminate according to gender. Thousands of young beautiful black, professional women—including the editor of this book—have plenty of horror stories that happen on a regular basis to them trying to catch a cab.

And racial profiling in the taxi industry isn't just about catching a cab—or the inability to catch one. One woman in her mid-thirties had trouble one year when she stepped into a cab and told the driver her destination—Roosevelt Island, located in the East River across from the Upper East Side and New York Hospital. It meant that the driver had to cross the Queensborough Bridge at Fifty-ninth Street, go through the Queensbridge Projects, cross a smaller Roosevelt Island bridge, and drop her off in front of her building on Main Street. This particular driver, a young immigrant from the Middle East, didn't want to go through the trouble.

"No, no!" he said, "I'm not going into Queens. It's too far. I'm about to end my shift."

"That doesn't have anything to do with me," the woman answered, closing the car door behind her. "I'm in your cab, and I told you where I want to go. You have to take me."

"No, no, no." He put the car in park, switched on the overhead light, and turned to his passenger. "I'm not going. Find another car."

The black woman didn't let up. "Then you better call your supervisor, 'cause I'm not getting out. I know my rights, and I want to go to Roosevelt Island."

For the next twenty minutes the cabdriver and his passenger were at a stalemate. The driver radioed into his dispatcher, who ordered him to drive the car back to the garage. If it were a strategy to get his passenger out, it didn't work. The cabbie drove off with his passenger, parked his cab in front of the building on West Fifty-something Street, called someone outside to watch his car, and walked away.

The woman eventually abandoned the ride and flagged down another cab at the next corner, but the damage was already done. Her evening started out as a beautiful dinner with friends and family at a restaurant in Chinatown and ended with a horrible confrontation alone late at night at some dirty taxi garage. Every driver has his own reasons for not picking up black passengers, if that's how he lives. It would be irresponsible to suggest that all taxi drivers discriminate. But of those who do, the drivers recite a variety of reasons for refusing to pick up black passengers, either male or female. Some say they don't like picking up black people because they always want to go to Brooklyn, or Queens, or some remote out-of-the-way neighborhood where drivers believe they couldn't get a return fare back into Manhattan.

Other drivers have said:

"They [black people] don't tip very well."

"They're rude and loud."

"They don't respect my cab. They throw trash on my floor and write on my seats."

The reasons they racially profile black customers can go

back a lifetime. But in the end, it boils down to the driver, many of whom are immigrants from countries with virtually no black citizens, who arrive in America with preconceived notions about black and Latino people. As one immigrant driver reported, many get their perceptions of black people from American movies and television and news programs that always portray black people as criminals. Black people, particularly young black men, are always depicted in a negative light or as wannabe gangsters or just all-out poor. They don't have money, or food for all their babies, so they rob and steal to get it. That was one driver's take.

One black woman provided this unsolicited comment: "They come from all over the world only to hear some really problematic, stereotypical things about African Americans, and those myths are never dispelled. That's why we can't get cabs. The underlying thing in all cases of racial profiling is stereotyping based on racist ideology that gets internalized by white people as well as people of color."

When this happens, it's more important than ever to provide racial-sensitivity training to dismantle these dangerous stereotypes—especially among taxi drivers.

What to Expect

In most cities around the country, there is a governing body that oversees taxis, limousines, buses, and any other public form of transportation. Usually it's here that you file a complaint. Check your local listings for the one in your city. In New York, the Taxi and Limousine Commission is where customers go to file a complaint against a taxi driver. You can file a complaint with the TLC in person at 40 Rector Street, New York, NY 10006, or over the phone at the twenty-four-hour TLC Consumer hotline, (212) NYC-TAXI. Filing a complaint with the TLC is relatively simple. All you need is (if possible) the name of the cabdriver, the medallion number of the cab, and time to appear at a hearing in which you will testify against the driver. (The name of the driver and medallion number are prominently posted on the dashboard of every taxi.) Once a complaint is filed, a hearing date is set. You appear to testify and answer any questions regarding your charges. Depending on the evidence and testimony, the driver will be issued a fine, or his hack license will be suspended (or revoked), or the case will be dismissed entirely.

A New York City Taxi Rider's Bill of Rights

- Direct destination and route used
- A courteous, English-speaking driver who knows the streets in Manhattan and the way to major out-of-borough destinations
- A driver who knows and obeys all traffic laws
- Air-conditioning on demand
- A radio-free (and silent) trip
- Smoke- and incense-free air
- A clean passenger-seat area
- A clean trunk
- Refuse a tip if any of the above are not complied with.

BIBLIOGRAPHY

- "Glover Says Cabs Won't Pick Him Up," by Salvatore Arena (*Daily News,* November 4, 1999) p. 5.
- " 'Lethal Weapon' Star Rips Apple's 'Racist' Cabbies," by Neil Graves, Rocco Parascandola, and Carl Campanile (*New York Post,* November 4, 1999) p. 14.
- "Danny Glover Says Cabbies Discriminated Against Him," by Monte Williams (*New York Times,* November 4, 1999) p. B8.
- "After Complaints by Actor, Group Will Sue Taxi Panel," by Thomas J. Lueck (*New York Times:* Metro Section, November 4, 1999) p. 38.
- "Taxi Raps Dropped," by Michael Finnegan and Pete Donohue (*Daily News,* November 10, 1999) p. 7.
- "For Racist Slights, the Meter is Still Running," by Felicia R. Lee (*New York Times:* City Section, November 28, 1999) Section 14; p. 1.

CHAPTER 18

In the News

There are not enough days in the millennium to write *Everything There Is to Know About Racial Profiling: The Encyclopedia.* The best this book can offer is a basic understanding of the concept. We've included people who have been victims, and empowered our readers by showing how other victims have handled racial profiling. But the premise of this book is to say that every person of color has a story of racial profiling to tell. In this chapter, we (with resources from the ACLU) share with readers a few lead paragraphs from various articles published around the country in 1999 in both mainstream and community presses, the *New York Times,* and a New Jersey newspaper, the *Newark Star-Ledger.*

New York Times, **November 18, 1999**

"Ad Executive Cites Her Race in Airport Search," by Winnie Hu

A black advertising executive accused United States Customs officers yesterday of subjecting her to an extensive pat-down search for drugs at Newark International Airport solely because of her race.

"I should have worn my blond wig and blue contacts and I probably wouldn't have been stopped," she said.

New York Times, **July 15, 1999**

"Near Detroit, a Familiar Sting in Being a Black Driver," by Robyn Meredith

DETROIT, July 15—The yuppie couple were driving home through the suburbs of Royal Oak after dinner and a movie when a police car behind them turned on its lights and siren.

Despite politely asking why they had been stopped, Mr. Archer said he and his date were ordered out of the car without explanation.

Crain's New York Business, **April 19–25, 1999**

"Always Under Police Suspicion," by Valerie Block and Matthew Goldstein

Earl "Butch" Graves Jr., 37, who was yanked off a Metro-North commuter train in 1995 by police officers looking for a black suspect, has had more recent encounters. Mr. Graves—son of the media baron who owns *Black Enterprise,* and the magazine's president—says he has been stopped while driving his Lexus in Manhattan on two occasions in the past year. He says that if you're black, "driving a Lexus is a recipe for disaster."

NBC's *Dateline*

The *Dateline* program reported on a case that reached national exposure when a Florida jury agreed with twenty-six-year veteran Florida police officer Aaron Campbell, who said he had been stopped on the Florida Turnpike because he was black. He was driving a late-model car heading north from Miami when he said he fit the racial profile of what many Florida cops were looking for in the fight against drug trafficking. Officer Campbell was pulled over for changing lanes without signaling, and later charged for driving with an obscured license plates, resisting arrest, and assaulting a police officer.

Emerge magazine, June 1999

"Traffic Violation," by Marci Davis

Police Major Aaron Campbell Jr. was heading north on the Florida Turnpike one evening when it happened to him.

Charles and Etta Carter were driving through Maryland, returning home to Philadelphia on their 40th wedding anniversary when it happened to them.

In each case, "it" is DWB—Driving While Black.

Emerge magazine, May 1999

"The Scales of Injustice," by Joe Davidson

[A young man named] Irving was a block away from his Oakland, Calif., home after grocery shopping on the evening of January 30 when he was stopped by a police officer for running a red light.

"When the policeman pulled me over, he immediately began to put handcuffs on me."

Emerge magazine, May 1999
"Race Matters," by Lottie L. Joiner

In Jasper, Ala., police are conducting traffic stops of whites who are driving in black areas.

Mayor Don Goetz ordered police to stop whites in two predominantly black neighborhoods at the request of residents who say whites "are causing the drug problem."

Esquire magazine, April 1999
"DWB: Driving While Black," by Gary Webb

You may have noticed that many of the motorists pulled over on the side of the highway are black or Hispanic. You may have attributed this to some kind of unspoken law-enforcement racism. You may be surprised to learn that it's the result of a federal program called Operation Pipeline, your tax dollars at work.

The Bergen Record, June 11, 1999
"Retired Cop's Suit Accuses Troopers of Improper Arrest," by David Voreacos

A lawyer for a retired New York City police officer Thursday alleged that the New Jersey State Police use gas station workers to gather information about black and Hispanic drivers.

Attorney Randolph M. Scott-McLaughlin said the arrest of James Powell on the New Jersey Turnpike suggests gas station attendants were helping troopers select minority motorists for enforcement action.

Newark Star-Ledger, June 15, 1999

"Minority Troopers Bolt Union, Charging Racism," by Kathy Barrett Carter

A group of 70 African American and Latino New Jersey state troopers are defecting from the State Police union, saying its leader is bigoted and sexist and that racism within the ranks is unrelenting from top to bottom.

Star-Ledger, June 16, 1999

"Pike Shooting Victims Tell Their Side to Jury," by Michael Raphael

The three minority men shot by state troopers on the New Jersey Turnpike 14 months ago testified yesterday before a state grand jury that will soon decide whether to bring criminal charges against the officers.

Their appearance signaled that prosecutors are close to wrapping up the grand jury investigation.

Star-Ledger, May 19, 1999

"Class-Action Suit Out of Philadelphia Cites Profiling," by Michael Raphael

A team of high-powered civil rights lawyers from Philadelphia has filed a federal class-action lawsuit accusing the New Jersey State Police of illegally targeting minority motorists for stops on the New Jersey Turnpike.

New York Times, May 19, 1999
"Hartford Chief Says Racism on His Force Must End," by Mike Allen

HARTFORD, May 18—With racial tensions rising after the fatal shooting last month of a black teenager by a white police officer, the Hartford police chief said today that he had become convinced that his force was infected with racism. He urged white officers to take steps to change their mind-set.

Star-Ledger, May 1, 1999
"Typical Pike Arrest: Black and Out of State," by Michael Raphael and Joe Donohue

He's 30 years old. He's black. He's got out-of-state license plates. And he's somewhere near Interchange 18W on the New Jersey Turnpike.

Those are the vital statistics—a profile, so to speak—of the typical motorist arrested by state troopers on the Turnpike between April 1997 and March 1998.

Star-Ledger, May 26, 1999
"Questions Mounting in Arrests on Pike," by Michael Raphael and Jim O'Neill

A year ago 22-year-old Timothy Gore was busted on the New Jersey Turnpike allegedly holding 17 ounces of cocaine.

Today a Superior Court judge is expected to drop those charges as well as charges against 20 other motorists accused of a variety of drug offenses by state troopers John Hogan and James Kenna.

Star-Ledger, **May 25, 1999**

"Former Top Trooper Admits Misconduct," by Guy Sterling

A former state police "Trooper of the Year" pleaded guilty yesterday to official misconduct on charges he shook down drivers on the New Jersey Turnpike, all but ending his career in law enforcement.

Star-Ledger, **April 21, 1999**

"For Downcast Troopers, Report Is No Surprise," by P. L. Wyckoff and Dan Weissman

There was anger and grim frustration among state troopers yesterday afternoon as news of the state's report on racial profiling spread among the ranks. . . .

One officer stationed at the Turnpike's Newark barracks said the constant barrage of controversy and criticism over the past year has taken a heavy toll on morale at a force that always has prided itself on being the state's elite.

New York Times, **April 2, 1999**

"Views on State Police Sharply Divided by Race"

TRENTON—Views on whether the state police do a good job and on whether troopers engage in racial profiling are sharply divided by race.

While 73 percent of whites polled said they approve of the performance of the state police and 16 percent said they disapproved, only 22 percent of blacks said they approved and 66 percent said they disapproved.

New York Times, **April 3, 1999**

"Top Giuliani Aide Said to Experience Race Bias by Police," by Dan Barry and Kevin Flynn

At the height of the public furor over the police shooting of Amadou Diallo, Deputy Mayor Rudy Washington—the highest-ranking black member of the Giuliani administration—told Mayor Rudolph W. Giuliani that he had been harassed more than once by police officers for what he considered to be racial reasons.

Star-Ledger

"Turnpike Arrests: 73 percent minority," by Michael Raphael and Joe Donohue

Amid mounting evidence that some state troopers target minority drivers on the New Jersey Turnpike, the Attorney General's Office yesterday released new statistics showing that three of four drivers arrested on the highway are minorities.

The figures show that of 222 arrests made during April and May 1997, 163 or 73 percent were minority motorists.

New York Times, **April 13, 1999**

"Judge Disallows Seizure of Illegal Gun," by Benjamin Weiser

Amid a public debate over the tactics of New York City police officers, a federal judge in Manhattan has ruled that the police violated the rights of a man who was stopped, searched, and arrested in 1997 for carrying an illegal handgun and fake immigration papers.

Star-Ledger, **April 14, 1999**

"Minorities Describe Humiliation by State Police," by Brian Donohue

Striving to put a human face on statistics indicating New Jersey State Police disproportionately target blacks and Hispanics for traffic stops, lawmakers yesterday heard minority motorists from all corners of the state recount their own often emotional tales of humiliating roadside stops.

New York Times, **April 20, 1999**

"Trenton Charges 2 Troopers with Falsifying Race of Drivers," by David Kocieniewski

TRENTON, April 19—In the first official sign that the New Jersey State Police may have illegally singled out black and Hispanic motorists, the attorney general today announced the indictments of two troopers accused of falsifying documents to make it appear that some of the black motorists they had stopped were white.

New York Times, **April 21, 1999**

"Whitman Says Troopers Used Racial Profiling," by Iver Peterson

TRENTON, April 20—Gov. Christine Todd Whitman and her attorney general conceded today for the first time that some state troopers single out black and Hispanic drivers on the highway, and that once they were pulled over, they were more than three times as likely as whites to be subjected to searches.

Daily News, **April 21, 1999**

"Whitman to Put End to Profiling," by Owen Moritz

Gov. Christie Whitman yesterday acknowledged racial profiling by New Jersey state troopers and vowed reforms after the release of a report on state police practices.

USA Today, **April 20, 1999**

"Blacks Speak Out About Fear of Police Officers," by Kevin Johnson

Jerod Jordan's mother, Gloria Watts, bought her son a Neon sedan because she thought anything flashier might make police suspicious. "I wanted him to be able to drive without having a problem," Watts said.

New York Times, **April 27, 1999**

"Verniero Rejects Blame in Profiling Issue," by David Kocieniewski

TRENTON, April 26—Attorney General Peter G. Verniero insisted to a Senate committee today that he responded appropriately to racial profiling allegations against the New Jersey State Police. He testified that it would be unfair to hold him personally responsible for the hundreds of drivers who were subjected to discrimination during the two years.

New York Times, April 28, 1999

"City Is to Pay $2.7 Million in Beating Suit," by Benjamin Weiser

The Giuliani administration has agreed to pay $2.75 million to a man [Harold Dusenbury, 42, of Willingboro, New Jersey] who said he was beaten on his way to work by at least five police officers because he fit the profile of a black suspect they were seeking.

Star-Ledger

"Feds Find Troopers Target Minority," by Michael Raphael

The U.S. Department of Justice has concluded that state police troopers have illegally targeted minority drivers for traffic stops on the New Jersey Turnpike since at least 1995 and yesterday said it would sue the agency to end the practice.

The determination is the result of a three-year investigation.

Star-Ledger, April 28, 1999

"Hotel Staffs Serve As Troopers' Eyes," by Kathy Barrett Carter and Kinga Borondy

A state police undercover operation that uses desk clerks to spot possible drug dealers in hotels and motels along the New Jersey Turnpike is being reviewed by the attorney general to determine whether it encourages racial profiling.

Star-Ledger, **April 19, 1999**

"San Diego Tracking Race in Traffic Stops," by Joe Donohue

San Diego Police Chief Jerry Sanders has a blunt answer to the question of whether police officers stop drivers solely because of their race:

Let's find out.

In February, Sanders ordered his department to begin tracking and making regular public reports on traffic stops.

New York Times, **March 27, 1999**

Metro News Briefs: "Trooper Suing State Says Vandals Hit His Home"

MOUNT HOLLY—County prosecutors are investigating whether someone vandalized the home of a New Jersey state trooper who filed a lawsuit last month against the state police, claiming he was forced by his superiors to stop drivers based on their race.

Star-Ledger, **February 28, 1999**

"Trooper Boss: Race Plays Role in Drug Crimes," by Joe Donohue

The superintendent of the New Jersey State Police says he has told all of his troopers that racial profiling will not be condoned, but he adds that he believes most of the illegal cocaine and marijuana business in the United States is conducted by minorities.

Daily News, **February 5, 1999**

"Fusillade Kills Bronx Peddler," by Rafael A. Olmeda and John Marzulli

An unarmed Bronx man was gunned down at close range yesterday by four plainclothes cops who fired 41 bullets—prompting a criminal investigation by the Bronx district attorney.

Amadou Diallo, 22, was pronounced dead at the scene, his bullet-riddled body crumpled faceup in the well-lighted vestibule of his building.

New York Times, **February 8, 1999**

"1,000 Rally to Condemn Shooting of Unarmed Man by Police," by Ginger Thompson

Charging "no justice, no peace" and saying the time may have come to "fight back," almost 1,000 people staged an angry rally yesterday on a snowy street in front of the Bronx home of a 22-year-old merchant [Amadou Diallo] gunned down in a storm of 41 bullets by four New York City police officers.

New York Times, **March 16, 1999**

"Dinkins Among 14 Arrested in Protest of Police Shooting," by Michael Cooper

Former Mayor David N. Dinkins, Representative Charles B. Rangel and 12 others were arrested yesterday as they staged a protest at Police Headquarters in lower Manhattan over the police killing of Amadou Diallo.

[Thousands of people would participate in the protest. They included Ossie Davis and Ruby Dee, *Black Enterprise* publisher Earl G. Graves and *Essence* publisher Ed Lewis, actress Susan Sarandon, among many, many others. Rev. Al Sharpton, head of the National Action Network, spearheaded the protest following the Diallo shooting.]

New York Times, **March 2, 1999**

"After Firing Chief, Whitman Defends Actions on Troopers," by David Kocieniewski

TRENTON, March 1—A day after firing the head of the New Jersey State Police for what she called racially insensitive remarks, Gov. Christine Todd Whitman today defended her administration's response to charges that state troopers single out black and Hispanic drivers in searching for drug traffickers.

New York Times, **March 23, 1999**

"Police May Have Understated Street Searches, Spitzer Says," by Richard Pérez-Peña

An elite police unit that includes the four officers who shot Amadou Diallo may have vastly underreported the number of people it has stopped and searched on the streets in the last two years, State Attorney General Eliot L. Spitzer said in a radio interview broadcast yesterday.

New York Times, **March 26, 1999**

"Caucus Plans Meetings on Racial Profiling"

TRENTON—The Black and Latino Caucus of the State Legislature announced yesterday that it would hold public meetings in April to look into allegations that the New Jersey State Police stop drivers based on their race.

New York Times, **March 24, 1999**
"Three Troopers' Unions Disavow Racial Profiling"

TRENTON—Amid accusations that the state police stop drivers based on their race, three unions representing troopers [State Troopers Fraternal Organization, the State Troopers Noncommissioned Officers Association, and the Troopers Superior Officers Association] have issued a statement of disavowing the practice.

CHAPTER 19

A Walk in the Park

A SENSE OF HUMOR

Herb Boyd is a longtime journalist who lives in Harlem. He remembers not too long ago having the kind of encounter in Central Park that many black men have experienced at one point or another during their lifetimes. As dusk fell over New York City, Herb was walking through a wooded area of the park, just off the beaten path located up near the East Seventies. In the distance about two hundred feet or so ahead of him, he spotted a young white couple in their late thirties or early forties headed toward him. They were elegantly dressed, as though they were on their way to an evening affair. And if they weren't, they were out for a stroll. The gentleman walked along the edge of the pathway, his companion to his side. A projected course would have Herb passing directly next to the woman.

For Herb, it was a nice day for a crosstown walk. The sky was clear, the air fresh. Although it was January, midwinter of 1998, the weather was exceptionally warm. Herb didn't see the couple any differently than any other couple (black or white). Then he noticed the woman looking hard. Central Park has had its notoriety over the years. In recent years alone, one woman reported to the New York City Police Department that a black man had robbed her of her money and jewelry, and a family touring the city with their young child reported that a black man had held a sharp unknown object to the their child's neck and demanded valuables. And everyone has heard about the Central Park Jogger who was beaten into a coma by a group of young black kids. It seems that to everyone who's ever had an image of a mugger in Central Park, it's always been of a black man.

Apparently this couple was no exception, because Herb could recognize the apprehension in the woman's face. No one else was around right then but she, her escort, and the black man wearing Levi's and a dark jacket. Herb must have been exuding a 1990s version of the hard-core black-nationalist with a "kill-whitey" attitude because as the couple got closer, Herb recognized suspicion in her eyes. Then he saw the inevitable: She shifted to the other side of her escort, and when they got to within fifty feet, she held him a little tighter, hooking her arm into his. It reminded Herb of the proverbial elevator where white women clutched their purses a little tighter when a black man entered.

But Herb wasn't a black youth. He was a prominent college professor, a prolific journalist, and the esteemed editor of the bestseller *Brother: The Odyssey of Black Men in*

America, edited by Herb Boyd and Robert L. Allen (One World/Ballantine Books, 1995). He keeps his salt-and-pepper hair neatly tucked beneath a khufia hat, and his mustache and beard well groomed. But can't a middle-class black American man who usually keeps his shoes polished, his pants ironed and his shirts neatly pressed take a moment to throw on some jeans and walk through the park without being racially profiled?

At first Herb thought to play into their stereotype and walk toward them with a scowl and a hard look. At the very least, he would get a chuckle out of seeing them cower away, having had their little scare for the evening. It would give them something to talk about. But he changed his mind. Instead, he toyed with the woman in another way, reminiscent of something James Baldwin had done when he encountered a frightened stranger on the street. As the couple walked to within twenty feet—and because the woman still maintained a frightened look in her eyes—Herb surprised them both.

"Hello." Herb smiled. "How are you doing?"

The couple lit up with laughter, especially the woman.

Herb laughed loudest.

There was no conversation. No chitchat or small talk. They all continued on their way, but when they got about fifty feet beyond one another, Herb looked over his shoulder and caught the couple looking back at him, too. And again they all laughed, sharing a brief moment that Herb hoped would be a learning experience for the couple.

BLACK HISTORY TRIVIA

- The first African American to graduate from West Point Military Academy was Henry O. Flipper of Georgia. He was admitted on July 1, 1873, and graduated on June 15, 1877. In 1999, President Bill Clinton gave Flipper a Presidential Pardon for his dishonorable discharge, which was believed to be racially motivated.
- On October 16, 1940, President Franklin Delano Roosevelt appointed Benjamin O. Davis, Sr., the first African American general in the U.S. Army.
- On October 27, 1954, Davis's son, Benjamin O. Davis, Jr., was appointed the first black general in the U.S. Air Force. In 1970, he retired with the rank of lieutenant general.
- In 1989, President George Bush named Gen. Colin L. Powell the first African American chairman of the Joint Chiefs of Staff. He would later lead the combined U.S. forces into combat during Desert Storm.
- In 1969, the residents of Cleveland, Ohio, elected Carl Stokes as the first African American mayor of a major metropolitan city.

BIBLIOGRAPHY

- *The African American Network,* by Crawford B. Bunkley (Plume, 1996).

Appendix

This chapter is designed to provide a resource list of proactive national organizations dedicated to fighting racism and racial profiling. There are many more organizations—national, mainstream, grassroots, niche, and on the Internet—that are not listed. (It would be nearly impossible for me to keep up. I'd need my own agency to track them.) The names appearing in this list are proven, legitimate, and fairly well known. Read your local newspaper. Keep up with other cases of racial profiling as they happen. As a reader, you have to look for the stories. They seldom make it onto the six-o'clock news. And for every one story that does, there are—by my own professional guess—ten more victims.

PROACTIVE ORGANIZATIONS

- ACLU (American Civil Liberties Union), 125 Broad Street, New York, NY 10004. (212) 549-2500.
- Center for Constitutional Rights, 666 Broadway, 7th floor, New York, NY 10012. (212) 614-6464.
- CORE (Congress of Racial Equality), 817 Broadway, New York, NY 10003. (212) 598-4000.
- Leadership Conference on Civil Rights, 1629 K. Street, N.W., Suite 1010, Washington, D.C. 20006. (202) 466-3311.
- ADL (Anti-Defamation League of B'nai B'rith), 823 United Nations Plaza, New York, NY 10017. (212) 490-2525. The ADL is one of the oldest Jewish organizations in the United States. Formed in 1913 specifically to battle anti-Semitism in the United States at the time, the ADL's battle evolved into a wider one to fight racism in all its forms. Around the campfire, it's been said that the ADL helped to create and finance the NAACP.
- SCLC (Southern Christian Leadership Conference), 334 Auburn Avenue, NE, Atlanta, GA 30303. (404) 522-1420.
- National Urban League (NUL), 120 Wall Street, New York, NY 10005. (212) 558-5300.
- National Action Network, 1941 Madison Avenue, 2nd floor, New York, NY 10035. (212) 987-5020.
- NAACP Legal Defense and Education Fund, 99 Hudson Street, New York, NY 10013. (212) 219-1900.
- National NAACP, 4805 Mount Hope Drive, Baltimore, MD 21215. (410) 358-8900.

- Amnesty International USA, 322 Eighth Avenue, New York, NY 10001. (212) 807-8400.
- Human Rights Campaign Fund, 919 Eighteenth Street, N.W., No. 800, Washington, D.C. 20006. (202) 628-4160.
- New York Offices of the Human Rights Watch, 350 Fifth Avenue, 34th floor, New York, NY 10118. (212) 290-4700. The Human Rights Watch conducts regular, systematic investigations of human-rights abuses in some seventy countries around the world. It addresses the human-rights practices of governments of all political stripes, of all geopolitical alignments, and of all ethnic and religious persuasions. It began in 1978 and remains an independent, nongovernmental organization supported by contributions from private individuals and foundations.
- Washington, D.C., Offices of Human Rights Watch, 1522 K. Street, N.W., No. 910, Washington, D.C. 20005-1202. (202) 371-6592.
- California Offices of the Human Rights Watch, 333 South Grant Street, Suite 430, Los Angeles, CA 90071. (213) 680-9906.

FEDERAL GOVERNMENT

Department of Housing and Urban Development
451 Seventh Street, S.W.
Washington, D.C. 20410
(202) 708-1112

Region II, HUD Regional Office
26 Federal Plaza
New York, NY 10278-0068
(212) 264-8000

U.S. Information Agency
301 Fourth Street, S.W.
Washington, D.C. 20547
(202) 619-4700

U.S. Information Agency
c/o New York City Offices
Educational & Cultural Affairs
New York Reception Center
666 Fifth Avenue
New York, NY 10103
(212) 399-5750

Department of Justice
Constitution Avenue and Tenth Street, N.W.
Washington, D.C. 20530
(202) 514-2000

Department of Justice
Community Relations Service
Headquarters Office
5550 Friendship Boulevard, Suite 330
Chevy Chase, MD 20815
(301) 492-5990

Federal Bureau of Investigation
Pennsylvania Avenue at Ninth Street, N.W.
Washington, D.C. 20535
(202) 324-3000

National Transportation Safety Board
490 L'Enfant Plaza East, S.W.
Washington, D.C. 20594
(202) 314-6000

Department of Transportation
400 Seventh Street, S.W.
Washington, D.C. 20590
(202) 366-4000

Federal Highway Administration
Washington Headquarters, Nassif Building
400 Seventh Street, S.W.
Washington, D.C. 20590
(202) 366-4000

National Highway Traffic Safety Administration
400 Seventh Street, S.W.
Washington, D.C. 20590
(202) 366-1836

Federal Transit Administration
400 Seventh Street, S.W.
Washington, D.C. 20590
(202) 366-4040

MISCELLANEOUS

Blacks in Government
1820 Eleventh Street, N.W.
Washington, D.C. 20001
(202) 667-3280

National Organization of Black Law Enforcement
   Executives
4609 Pinecrest Office Park Drive, Suite F
Alexandria, VA 23312
(703) 658-1529 or (703) 914-2169

National Black Police Association
3251 Mount Pleasant Street, N.W.
Washington, D.C. 20010
(202) 986-2070

Acknowledgments

When my agent, Marie Brown, introduced me to Double-day editor Deborah Cowell with the assignment to write a book on racial profiling, I had no idea how widespread the problem was. I had heard, here and there, about New Jersey police officers pulling over young black men, but I considered those isolated events. I was dead wrong! Immediately, as I put together a snapshot of racial profiling on a personal, national, and institutional level, I discovered that everyone had a story to tell, and just as many people had two.

But don't get me wrong, I recognize a legitimate stop. I was once stopped in Kentucky doing ninety miles an hour. When the officer asked me why I was going so fast, I confessed that my wife and I were trying to get to a party in Washington, D.C. That was a legitimate stop. But as a teenager, one night I was picking up the family car over on Roosevelt Island, New York, when the island's security patrol and two police officers surrounded me, their flashing squad lights and bright lights helping to make their interrogation dramatic. They thought I was trying to steal the car.

Racial profiling is a real problem, and I'm not just talking about law-enforcement agencies. Let's not focus only on the police. Racial profiling takes place everywhere: department stores, restaurant counters, airport terminals, and grocery stores. In Florida just before Thanksgiving 1999, a restaurant owner was ordered to pay $15 million and have his employees undergo sensitivity training. The company settled a lawsuit over the fact they were charging a 15 percent gratuity directly to the check of black patriots and not whites. When the manager was informed, he said, "It was added because you black people don't tip well."

As I've said before, there are not enough days in a century to write *The Complete Book on Racial Profiling: The Encyclopedia*. Just to write this book took the resources of a lot of people. And I want to give thanks to everyone.

I thank Debbie Cowell for the concept and Marie Brown for recommending me to write it. I called Marie Brown every day for a year, trying to break into the book-publishing world. Who says persistence doesn't pay off?

To my mother and father, I thank you for my life and raising me to be a productive citizen in society. Also to my wife, Glenna, and my three children; my sister; my three brothers; my nieces; and my nephews, especially the rising filmmaker Damani Higgins. Jah bless you and your respective families.

To everyone who allowed me to tell the world their stories: I say thank you to New York photographer Samuel

Elijah and *Black Enterprise* art director Terence Saulsby for their stories. Many more thanks go out to Amy Bowllan and her family; Howie Evans and his family; Christopher Thomas and his family; and Det. Clifton Hollingsworth, Jr., and his family. Special thanks go out to the support from Reginald Shuford, staff attorney for the American Civil Liberties Union, and Robert Wilkins, whose case unveiled the problem of racial profiling among the Maryland State Police Department. Thanks also go out to the people who remain nameless, yet whose ideas and concepts had a unique influence in the shaping of this book.

I also have to give thanks to everyone behind the scenes, people who were equally instrumental in getting this book together and yet whose names appear only on this page. Great thanks especially go to Dawn Ward, Esq., who kept me informed of all the legal conferences in town that dealt with the subject of racial profiling. Also deserving of great thanks are former *Newark Star-Ledger* reporter Terri P. Guess, who forwarded relevant articles that helped me to understand the subject, and Howard Amos, who also sent me relevant articles from the South and who offered a little insight into the life of a security guard.

I also want to thank my former editors, who have helped me professionally in my career: Elinor Tatum, publisher and editor-in-chief of the *New York Amsterdam News*; Sonia Alleyne, editor-in-chief of *Black Elegance* and *Belle* magazines; Carolyn A. Butts, publisher and former partner at *African Voices*; Alfred A. Edmond, Jr., senior vice president and editor-in-chief at *Black Enterprise* magazine; Don Rojas, the former executive editor of the *New York Amsterdam News*; and Herb and Elza Boyd, book authors and prominent writers. Thanks to Herb Boyd for recommending me as managing editor to Sonia Alleyne. Thank you all for believing in me.

Forgive me if I'm leaving anyone's name out. If I did, there is probably a technical reason. In the meantime, I hope you enjoyed reading *Driving While Black: Highways, Shopping Malls, Taxicabs, Sidewalks—How to Fight Back If You Are a Victim of Racial Profiling*.

—Kenneth Meeks
New York, New York
May 2000